THE CHANGING SOVIET NAVY

Studies in Defense Policy
TITLES PUBLISHED

Naval Force Levels and Modernization:
An Analysis of Shipbuilding Requirements
Arnold M. Kuzmack

Support Costs in the Defense Budget: The Submerged One-Third
Martin Binkin

The Changing Soviet Navy
Barry M. Blechman

BARRY M. BLECHMAN

THE CHANGING SOVIET NAVY

A Staff Paper

THE BROOKINGS INSTITUTION
Washington, D.C.

Copyright © 1973 by
THE BROOKINGS INSTITUTION
1775 Massachusetts Avenue, N.W., Washington, D.C. 20036

Library of Congress Cataloging in Publication Data:
Blechman, Barry M
   The changing Soviet Navy.
   (Studies in defense policy, 3)
   Includes bibliographical references.
    1. Russia (1923–   U.S.S.R.). Voenno-Morskoĭ Flot.
I. Title. II. Series.
VA573.B55   359.3'0947   73-2881
ISBN 0-8157-0995-1 (pbk.)

THE BROOKINGS INSTITUTION is an independent organization devoted to nonpartisan research, education, and publication in economics, government, foreign policy, and the social sciences generally. Its principal purposes are to aid in the development of sound public policies and to promote public understanding of issues of national importance.

The Institution was founded on December 8, 1927, to merge the activities of the Institute for Government Research, founded in 1916, the Institute of Economics, founded in 1922, and the Robert Brookings Graduate School of Economics and Government, founded in 1924.

The Board of Trustees is responsible for the general administration of the Institution, while the immediate direction of the policies, program, and staff is vested in the President, assisted by an advisory committee of the officers and staff. The by-laws of the Institution state, "It is the function of the Trustees to make possible the conduct of scientific research, and publication, under the most favorable conditions, and to safeguard the independence of the research staff in the pursuit of their studies and in the publication of the results of such studies. It is not a part of their function to determine, control, or influence the conduct of particular investigations or the conclusions reached."

The President bears final responsibility for the decision to publish a manuscript as a Brookings book or staff paper. In reaching his judgment on the competence, accuracy, and objectivity of each study, the President is advised by the director of the appropriate research program and weighs the views of a panel of expert outside readers who report to him in confidence on the quality of the work. Publication of a work signifies that it is deemed to be a competent treatment worthy of public consideration; such publication does not imply endorsement of conclusions or recommendations contained in the study.

The Institution maintains its position of neutrality on issues of public policy in order to safeguard the intellectual freedom of the staff. Hence interpretations or conclusions in Brookings publications should be understood to be solely those of the author or authors and should not be attributed to the Institution, to its trustees, officers, or other staff members, or to the organizations that support its research.

FOREWORD

The U.S. Navy is in the midst of a major modernization program. The level of federal budget authorizations for naval construction has tripled since its fiscal 1969 low point; it is now 50 percent higher than its average from fiscal 1962 to 1969. Among the many factors that have combined to bring about this substantial increase is the greater emphasis that U.S. naval planners have placed on developments in Soviet naval capabilities. This paper—the third in Brookings' Studies in Defense Policy series—provides a starting point for assessing the origins, political implications, and future course of the U.S.-Soviet naval rivalry.

The author focuses on changes in the Soviet Navy since 1958—a turning point in the evolution of Soviet sea power. He finds that the improvement in Soviet naval capabilities cannot be ascribed to increasing force levels. On the contrary, the number of operational units in key components of the Soviet Navy has already been, or will soon be, sharply reduced. Growing capabilities, he argues, result from improvements in the performance of individual units, brought about particularly by the introduction of cruise missiles and nuclear power for submarines, and a broader definition of the peacetime role of Soviet warships.

After surveying the actual and potential missions of the Soviet fleet in an attempt to determine the relative emphasis Soviet leaders place on each, the author assesses possible future directions in Soviet naval evolution. His analysis reflects data concerning the construction of new vessels—including the Soviet Union's first aircraft carrier, now being built at the Nikolaev shipyard on the Black Sea—and recent writings by Soviet naval leaders. He emphasizes the Soviet Union's increasing propensity to use its navy for international political purposes.

Barry M. Blechman is a research associate in the Foreign Policy Studies program. Before coming to Brookings in 1971, he was on the staff of the Center for Naval Analyses.

The Institution thanks George H. Quester, Stanley R. Resor, and General Matthew B. Ridgway—members of its Defense Advisory Board—for their helpful comments on the manuscript. Others who gave generously of their time to comment include Brigadier General Arnold W. Braswell, Raymond L. Garthoff, Brigadier General Daniel O. Graham, Lieutenant General Glenn A. Kent, Vice Admiral John M. Lee, Michael K. MccGwire, Rear Admiral Robert R. Monroe, Robert C. Moot, Philip A. Odeen, Thomas R. Pickering, Vice Admiral Stansfield Turner, Admiral Maurice F. Weisner, and Thomas W. Wolfe. Mr. Blechman thanks Commander Ted Baker, Bruce C. Clarke, N. Bradford Dismukes, Robert W. Herrick, David B. Kassing, Anne M. Kelly, James M. McConnell, Henry Owen, and Robert G. Weinland for their comments and suggestions. He is also grateful to Gail L. Zirkel, who typed the manuscript, and to Susan Stone for her editorial assistance.

The Institution acknowledges the assistance of the Ford Foundation, whose grant helps to support its work in defense studies. The views expressed are solely those of the author and should not be ascribed to any of the persons named above who commented on the manuscript, to the Ford Foundation, or to the trustees, officers, or other staff members of the Brookings Institution.

KERMIT GORDON
President

March 1973
Washington, D.C.

CONTENTS

THE CHANGING SOVIET NAVY

In recent years the Soviet Navy has become a subject of considerable interest, widespread debate, and some worry in the United States. Much of this concern focuses on matters of mainly military import—the size and composition of the force, technical characteristics of weapons and sensor systems, ship performance, and so forth. In the broader policy arena, however, there is increasing concern about the implications of the changing Soviet Navy for the United States' ability to achieve its foreign policy objectives. Such concern figures prominently in testimony by Department of Defense officials in support of the Navy's budget and underlies much of the U.S. naval modernization program initiated in recent years.

The purpose of this paper is to aid in the evaluation of changes in Soviet naval capabilities. Developments in the military potential of the United States' most powerful potential adversary must, of course, be a major consideration in determining the military posture to be pursued by this nation. Nonetheless, a prudent response should consider not only the composition and capabilities of the Soviet fleets but also how they are likely to be used. The missions of the Soviet Navy, which reflect the USSR's conception of the military and political utility of sea power, constitute an important element for understanding the potential consequences of Soviet naval developments for the security of American interests.

On the other hand, comparisons of Soviet naval force levels with those of the United States, a frequently encountered method for analyzing Soviet naval development, constitute a relatively unimportant element in determining a prudent American response. Just as the two nations are very different entities —in their ideology, in their geographic situation, in their outlook on world affairs and military strategy, and in their interdependence with foreign nations for economic well-being—so too are their navies very different. Comparisons of the two fleets in numbers of ships, age, tonnage, expenditures, or manpower necessarily incorporate a number of simplifying (and often erroneous) assumptions or omissions. Such comparisons, for example, do not take into account the net capabilities of the fleets, which are determined, in part, by the manner in which they are postulated to interact. The U.S. and Soviet Navies have been designed by different hands with very different purposes and, as such, their differences far outweigh their similarities.

Since such comparisons may have political consequence and are cited frequently in debates concerning this topic, a brief discussion is appended to this paper which compares the two navies and describes possible scenarios in which they might enter into combat. The body of the paper, however, deliberately avoids this approach. The primary analysis is predicated upon very different grounds—a comparison of the present Soviet Navy with the Soviet Navy as it existed in 1958.

The base year 1958 has not been chosen capriciously, although 1957 or 1959 would provide equally valid benchmarks for the level of generalization to be undertaken. The process through which major items of military equipment are designed and procured is time-consuming. Consequently, considerable delays occur between decisions about the type of operations that should be undertaken by a navy (or any military service) and the weapons necessary to carry them out, and the actual appearance of these forces.[1]

The size and composition of the Soviet Navy today fundamentally are the result of decisions about economic priorities and military doctrine and strategy reached by Stalin's successors in the aftermath of his death (1953-54). At that time, drastic alterations were made in the massive rebuilding program instituted by Stalin in the late 1940s. Force level objectives were cut back dramatically, some shipbuilding programs were canceled altogether, new development programs were initiated, and others were given higher priority than they previously had received. Subsequent decisions led to modifications but not to basic changes in the naval program laid out in 1953-54.[2]

1. One informed observer has estimated that the following time lags are pertinent to Soviet decisions: (a) those that add equipment to existing vessels but do not require design changes, two to three years; (b) those that modify equipment so as to require modest design changes, five to six years; (c) those that require new ship designs but use many items already available, eight years; and (d) those requiring complete ship design from the ground up, ten to twelve years. Comments by Michael MccGwire, at a seminar on Soviet Naval Development, Maritime Workshop, Dalhousie University, Halifax, Nova Scotia, October 1972.

2. The principal study of the development of Soviet naval doctrine and capabilities is Robert W. Herrick, *Soviet Naval Strategy: Fifty Years of Theory and Practice* (U.S. Naval Institute, 1968). Additional information, particularly about decision periods in Soviet naval procurement, is given in Michael MccGwire, "Soviet Naval Capabilities and Intentions" (paper presented at the Royal United Service Institute conference, "The Soviet Union in Europe and the Near East," Milford-on-Sea, England, 1970); reprinted in *Congressional Record* (July 1, 1971), pp. 6850-58. Also Michael MccGwire, "Soviet Naval Procurement" (paper presented at RUSI conference, "The Soviet Union in Europe and the Near East"); reprinted in *Congressional Record* (July 1, 1971), pp. E6861-65.

The year 1958 is representative of the condition of the Soviet Navy just before the initial impact of the post-Stalin decisions began to be made manifest. It marked the first appearance of some naval vessels initiated in the 1946 building programs—namely, those that incorporated wartime and postwar design features. It was the year in which the first nuclear-powered submarines were delivered to the Soviet fleet, and the year in which Soviet warships armed with surface-to-surface cruise (air-breathing) missiles made their first public appearance. It also marked a point just before the Soviet Union began to retire large .numbers of older, less effective vessels and the beginning of a four-year halt in the construction of surface warships.

Thus, symbolically, 1958 serves as a watershed in the evolution of Soviet naval capabilities. It is assumed that the number, type, and characteristics of naval units acquired (and retired) during the interval between 1958 and 1973 reflect the evolution of Soviet thought about the utility of sea power. A comparison of the Soviet Navy of 1958 with the Soviet Navy today is intended to highlight the priorities that the Soviet Union places on the various missions that naval forces potentially can undertake and to describe the manner in which these priorities may have changed over time. Data pertaining to changing force levels and weapons characteristics will be supplemented with information regarding operations, exercises, and deployment patterns of Soviet naval forces.

In addition to a comparison of the Soviet Navy of 1958 and 1973, attention is given in this paper to recent indications that the Soviet Union may be in the process of rethinking the role of its navy or may recently have completed such an evaluation. Because of the delay between decision and deployment, noted previously, the results of such a reevaluation would not become apparent for several years. A later section will, therefore, consider these possibilities and describe potential directions and important indicators of new changes in Soviet naval priorities.

The Soviet Navy: "Old" and "New"

The Soviet Navy has changed a great deal since 1958. It is a more modern military force by contemporary standards and consequently far more capable in many respects. It is impressive in the extent of its modernization, in the performance of its new weapons, sensors, and other electronic equipment, and in the scope of its now-global deployments. At the same time, the Soviet Navy in 1973 is no larger than it was in 1958 and, in fact, is smaller in several key components. While to date the number of major surface warships has remained relatively constant, it has many fewer submarines and aircraft. Moreover, major surface warship and submarine force levels are likely to decline sharply in the near future. Overall, as indexed by manpower, the size of the Soviet Navy has diminished by about one-third (750,000 to 500,000).[3] While these manpower figures are only representative, being rough estimates from Western sources, the trend definitely has been in this direction. Perhaps greater significance can be invested in the 1968 reduction in the Soviet Navy's term of conscription from four to three years. Assuming that total manpower has not increased, such a move would have a significant effect on the number of men available for operational forces.

These declines in force levels should not be surprising. Under Stalin, the USSR long demonstrated a penchant for quantitative superiority, stemming from ideological, strategic, and geographic requirements. For example, at the outbreak of World War II, the Soviet Union had more tanks than the rest of the world combined, a larger air force and more airborne troops than any other nation, and more than twice the submarine force of Germany.[4] Given the steep cost increase associated with the development of technologically advanced weapon systems, the lengthy time periods necessary to build these weapons, and their requirement for technically proficient personnel, the maintenance of force levels in 1973 comparable to those in 1958 would have necessitated major increases in resources allocated to the Soviet Navy. Similar factors contributed to reduced force levels in the U.S. Navy—the total number of active ships declining from 890 in 1958 to 655 in 1972.[5] In short, the USSR, like the United States, has been compelled during the past fifteen years to trade quantity for quality in its naval forces. The following paragraphs will examine these trade-offs in more detail for various types of Soviet naval units.

Submarines

The submarine force (Table 1) has experienced a major decline in number of units. If ballistic missile submarines are excluded, according to *Jane's*, the force has diminished by more than 25 percent. It will decline to a greater

3. Raymond V. B. Blackman (ed.), *Jane's Fighting Ships, 1958-59* and *1972-73* (Jane's Yearbooks, 1958 and 1972).

4. James M. McConnell, "Ideology and Soviet Military Strategy," in Richard F. Staar (ed.), *Aspects of Modern Communism* (University of South Carolina Press, 1968).

5. *The Budget of the United States Government for the Fiscal Year Ending June 30, 1969*, p. 438; *Department of Defense Appropriations, Fiscal Year 1973*, Hearings before a Subcommittee of the Senate Committee on Appropriations, 92 Cong. 2 sess. (1972), Pt. 3, p. 24.

extent in the near future. The Soviet Union faces an obsolescence problem involving W-class submarines, which make up more than 40 percent of the 1972 force listed in the table. These submarines, built between 1950 and 1957, are being retired rapidly and are not being replaced on a one-for-one basis. Admiral Zumwalt has already listed the Soviet torpedo attack and cruise missile submarine force level as 288, more than 50 fewer than the number appearing in the table.[6]

Since 1968, the Soviet Union has been producing nuclear-powered submarines at the rate of 15 to 16 a year, 9 to 10 of which have been ballistic missile submarines.[7] If one assumes that all diesel-powered submarines built before 1958—W, W(mod), Q, and Z classes—will be retired by 1980 and that the construction rate of 16 a year will continue, in 1980 the Soviet Union will have a force of some 200 to 230 torpedo attack and cruise missile submarines. The exact force level will depend upon the ultimate number of ballistic missile submarines constructed, the disposition of other diesel-powered classes, and Soviet decisions about future construction rates for both nuclear- and diesel-powered units. In any case, the torpedo attack and cruise missile submarine force in 1980 will probably be less than one-half the size of the force in 1958; more than three-fourths of it, however, will be nuclear-powered.

This contrast between diminishing force levels but increasing capabilities for individual units is already apparent. While considerably smaller than in 1958, the Soviet submarine force is now more capable in many respects. The introduction of nuclear propulsion has been one element in these advances; 95 of the submarines listed in Table 1 are nuclear-powered, including strategic, cruise missile, and torpedo attack varieties. The introduction of cruise missiles

6. Letter, Admiral E. R. Zumwalt, Jr., to Senator William Proxmire, June 2, 1972, reprinted in *Congressional Record* (June 12, 1972), pp. S9186-92. (Cited hereafter as Zumwalt letter of June 2.) Force level data in the tables are drawn from *Jane's Fighting Ships, 1958-59* and *1972-73*. This annual publication is considered the most authoritative and comprehensive unclassified source on this subject. Exclusive dependence on *Jane's* permitted a more systematic comparison of the two years than would have been possible if diverse sources had been used.

On the other hand, the data in *Jane's* generally are not the most recent available. The latest edition, for example, which appeared in the summer of 1972, reflects estimates of the Soviet order of battle at around the beginning of the year and is thus one year old at the time of this writing. Moreover, there is a tendency in *Jane's* to err on the conservative side regarding the possible retirement of older vessels. Consequently, the text of the paper will supplement the data in the tables with more recent information, wherever this is relevant.

7. Michael MccGwire, "Current Soviet Warship Construction," in MccGwire (ed.), "Soviet Naval Development: Capability and Context" (Halifax: Maritime Workshop, Dalhousie University, 1973; processed), pp. 118-25.

Table 1. The Soviet Submarine Force, 1958 and 1972

Characteristic	Diesel-powered		Nuclear-powered	
	1958	*1972*	*1958*	*1972*
Torpedo attack and cruise missile submarines				
Number of units	474	286	(3)[a]	61
Mean tonnage[b]	0.8	1.3	3.5	4.4
Mean range[c]	9.5	14.5	∞	∞
Mean complement	43.7	61.6	88	95
Total number of torpedo tubes	2,478	1,808	18	400
Total number of cruise missiles				
(tubes or rails)	0	98	0	304
Strategic (ballistic missile) submarines				
Number of units	7[d]	25	0	34
Total number of missiles (tubes)	14	72	0	427
Mean tonnage[b]	2.1	2.6	–	6.9
Mean range[c]	20.0	23.1	–	∞

Sources: Force level data are taken from *Jane's Fighting Ships, 1958-59* and *1972-73.*
Data pertaining to ships' characteristics are derived from *Jane's* and Siegfried Breyer,
Guide to the Soviet Navy, translated by Lt. Cdr. M. W. Henley (U.S. Naval Institute,
1970).
  a. Three nuclear units were listed as under construction in 1958.
  b. Maximum surface displacement in thousands of tons.
  c. At cruising speed, in thousands of nautical miles.
  d. Derived from issues of *Jane's* after 1958-59.

themselves has been an important advance; 66 submarines were so equipped
in 1972. The implications of this measure are discussed in subsequent sections.

Aggregate submarine tonnage has grown by 50 percent despite the decline
in force levels. Similarly, the decline in the total number of torpedo tubes has
not been proportional to the decline in force levels, as new submarines incorporate more tubes per boat. The diesel-powered force alone is now more
capable, in some respects, than its 1958 counterpart. Table 1 shows a 53 percent increase in these units' mean range, which reflects a halt in the construction of coastal and medium-range units. Also, many short-range submarines of
prewar construction or design have been retired.

Major Surface Warships

A different trend has been experienced by the Soviet force of major surface warships (Table 2). In this case, force levels have remained fairly stable
but mean tonnage has diminished, reflecting a shift in the relative building
rates between escorts and large destroyers. The Soviet Union, however, has
retained a surprisingly large number of older gun cruisers in its active inventory. These vessels are apparently the ships in the Soviet Navy best suited to

Table 2. Soviet Major Surface Warships, 1958 and 1972

Characteristic	Cruisers[a]		Destroyers[b]		Escorts[c]		All major combatants	
	1958	1972	1958	1972	1958	1972	1958	1972
Number of units	31	29	146	101	66	124	243	254
Mean tonnage[d]	12.4	10.4	2.3	2.9	1.3	1.2	3.3	2.9
Mean complement[e]	932	760	260	299	168	124	321	265
Number of surface-to-surface missiles (rails)	0	72	0	16	0	0	0	88
Number of surface-to-air missiles (rails)	0	46	0	86	0	0	0	132
Number of torpedo tubes[f]	216	218	1,318	831	198	657	1,732	1,706
Number of anti-submarine rockets[g]	0	396	832	1,636	1,152	4,552	1,984	6,584
Helicopter capacity[h]	0	50	22	20	0	0	22	70
Mine capacity[e]	5,140	2,980	11,270	5,260	2,700	3,930	19,110	12,170

Sources: Force level data are taken from *Jane's Fighting Ships, 1958-59* and *1972-73*. Data pertaining to ships' characteristics are derived from *Jane's* and Breyer, *Guide to the Soviet Navy*.

a. Includes two Moskva-class helicopter cruisers in 1972.

b. As defined by *Jane's*.

c. Ocean-going escorts larger than 1,000 tons.

d. Standard displacement in thousands of tons.

e. Maximum listed.

f. The comparison of torpedo tubes is not really meaningful. The 1958 torpedos were anti-surface-ship weapons. The 1972 torpedos are chiefly designed for antisubmarine warfare.

g. Number of launcher barrels. Ships that may be outfitted with either depth charges or rockets are, for purposes of this table, assumed to be outfitted with rockets.

h. On-board maintenance, maximum capacity.

serve as command flagships, primarily because of their size (to accommodate command staffs and communications gear) and endurance.

The Soviet Union will face some difficulty maintaining present force levels in future years. It confronts an obsolescence problem in this category similar to, but of a lesser magnitude than, that in submarines. Nearly 20 percent of the 1972 force described in Table 2 is made up of Skoryi-class destroyers, which were built between 1949 and 1953. These vessels are becoming obsolescent, even though some of them were retrofitted with more modern antisubmarine warfare (ASW) systems between 1958 and 1961. Kotlin-class destroyers, an additional 10 percent of the 1972 force, were constructed between 1954 and 1957. The eventual retirement of these vessels should counteract the effect of new construction and result in decreasing force levels in the future.[8] This decline can only be avoided if the Soviet Union allocates

8. Admiral Zumwalt's letter of June 2 already listed twenty-five gun destroyers fewer than the number shown in Table 2.

greater resources to naval shipbuilding, either by reallocating civilian shipyards to naval construction or by building new shipyards. There is no evidence to date that such decisions have been made.[9]

The Soviet surface fleet, like the submarine force, is more capable than in 1958, even if no larger. A large portion of the force is composed of ships of relatively recent vintage; 50 percent of the cruisers, 40 percent of the destroyers, and 50 percent of the escorts have become operational since 1958. These newer units, despite their smaller average size, pack greater firepower on more diversified systems, are speedier, and carry more elaborate and sophisticated electronic equipment. The Russians seem to have made major advances in surface ship design and engineering efficiency. Ton for ton, the newest Soviet destroyer—the Krivak—is said to be the most powerful warship ever built.[10]

The introduction of missile systems has been of particular importance in developing the capabilities of Soviet surface units. The 1972 force included twenty vessels armed with surface-to-surface missiles and nearly forty armed with surface-to-air missiles.[11] The Soviet Union also seems to have made considerable improvement in its antisubmarine capabilities with the introduction of new sonars and torpedos, ship-borne helicopters, and large numbers of antisubmarine rockets. Only mine capacity seems to have declined substantially.

Other Forces

Comparative data for other components of the Soviet Navy are found in Table 3. The following should be noted.

Coastal escorts and other patrol vessels (submarine chasers and so forth) have nearly doubled in number but decreased in tonnage since 1958. Three-fourths of the ships of this type have been built since 1958. Although the newer ships are smaller than their predecessors, their weaponry is relatively more impressive.

There has been a considerable decline in the number of torpedo boats and gunboats. Introduction of missile-equipped patrol vessels has been a compensating trend, however, The Nanuchka, a missile corvette, is an important recent addition to the missile patrol boat grouping.

9. MccGwire, "Current Soviet Warship Construction." It should be noted that one of the main consequences of the 1954 decisions was to shift a considerable portion of naval shipbuilding capability to the construction of merchant, fishing, and other civilian-oriented shipping.

10. Zumwalt letter of June 2, p. 6.

11. These categories are not mutually exclusive; twelve vessels have both types of missiles.

Table 3. Other Soviet Naval Forces, 1958 and 1972

Type and characteristic	1958	1972
Coastal escorts and other patrol vessels[a]		
Number of units	133	258
Mean tonnage[b]	361	287
Number of surface-to-air missiles (rails)	0	16
Number of torpedo tubes	75	632
Number of antisubmarine rockets (barrels)	0	3,728
Mine capacity[c]	2,690	3,000
Missile patrol boats		
Number of units	0	151
Number of surface-to-surface missiles (rails)	0	566
Motor torpedo/gun boats		
Number of units[d]	500	225
Amphibious warfare vessels[e]		
Number of units	120	200
Mean tonnage[b]	350	800
Minesweepers		
Oceangoing (number of units)	149	189
Coastal and inshore (number of units)	161	130
Naval aviation		
Number of aircraft	3,000	1,200

Sources: Force level data are taken from *Jane's Fighting Ships, 1958-59* and *1972-73*. Data pertaining to ships' characteristics are derived from *Jane's* and Breyer, *Guide to the Soviet Navy.*

a. All surface warships other than those already listed, including coastal escorts, fast escorts, patrol vessels, and submarine chasers.

b. Standard displacement in tons.

c. Maximum capacity if normally carried.

d. Excluding river craft.

e. Including amphibious craft.

Growth has been experienced in both force levels and tonnage in the amphibious and mine warfare categories. It should be added, however, that amphibious warfare is one area which the Soviet Union has neglected sorely. This is discussed further in a subsequent section. The USSR has also neglected the development of support ships, a category for which publicly available data are too spotty to present quantitative measures. Generally, their support forces have made do with civilian ships conscripted for naval use.[12] What new construction there has been in the support area has tended to focus on the support of submarines. The Soviet Navy is just beginning to develop a significant capability to refuel and provide other types of logistical support to its

12. Siegfried Breyer, *Guide to the Soviet Navy,* translated by Lt. Cdr. M. W. Henley (U.S. Naval Institute, 1970), pp. 129-34.

ships at sea[13] and thus has no real equivalent to the U.S. Navy's underway replenishment groups.

Finally, Soviet naval aviation differs greatly from that of 1958. The older force was composed in large part of land-based interceptor squadrons, which were intended to be used for the defense of ports, bases, and fleet areas against air attacks. These units have been phased out or transferred to other branches of the Soviet military, primarily to the Air Defense Command (PVO Strany). In 1972, the much smaller naval air arm consisted of long-range Bear aircraft, primarily used for reconnaissance; medium-range strike aircraft, some equipped with cruise missiles, cast in an antiship role; and helicopters and fixed-wing aircraft designed for antisubmarine warfare. The naval air force of 1,200 aircraft continues to be land-based; only a small number of helicopters fly from Soviet cruisers and destroyers.[14]

What Has Changed?

The Soviet Navy has become a topic of general interest in the United States only since 1967. What has happened to cause this sudden prominence? As we have seen, there has not been a major increase in the size of the Soviet Navy; rather, the reverse has occurred. Nor for that matter can the new interest simply be the result of the sudden appearance of more modern ships. After all, in 1958 more than 40 percent of the Soviet submarine force had become operational within the previous seven years; the comparable statistic in 1972 was only 30 percent. Similarly, in 1958 three-fourths of the Soviet Union's major surface warships were less than eight years old; in 1972 this proportion was roughly one-fourth.

Much of the new prominence of Soviet naval capabilities may be attributed to developments in the United States and other Western nations rather than to changes in the Soviet Navy itself. That is, decreases in Western naval force levels may have caused the relative balance of naval power to appear to be shifting in a direction favorable to the Soviet Union. Or various Western governmental and private groups may have perceived it to be in their interest or may have been led by internal developments to place added emphasis on developments in Soviet naval capabilities. To the degree that the renewed Western interest in the Soviet Navy is the result of developments in the Soviet Navy itself, however, two factors seem to be of foremost importance: (a)

13. See Zumwalt letter of June 2, p. 14.
14. *Jane's Fighting Ships, 1972-73*, p. 577.

striking improvements in the capabilities of individual units and (b) a sharp change in the Soviet Navy's peacetime deployment patterns.

Advances in Unit Capabilities

The previous section referred to many improvements in the capabilities of individual units. These need not be repeated here. In two areas, however, advances in platforms and weapon systems have resulted in the attainment of completely new capabilities.

First, deployment of Yankee-class submarines now gives the Soviet Union a credible, sea-based strategic missile force. As such, for the first time the Soviet Navy presents a direct threat to the continental United States. Although only twenty-five units were operational by January 1972, Yankees (or a modified version) were being constructed at the rate of nine to ten a year, and the initiation of construction of the forty-second such unit has already been reported.[15]

Second, the deployment of large numbers of cruise missiles, carried by submarines, aircraft, and some surface units gives the USSR an impressive anti-surface-ship capability. The sinking of the Israeli destroyer *Eilat* by Soviet-supplied naval missiles seems to have contributed more than any other single event to recent concern about the Soviet Navy. Symbolically, deployment of missile-equipped surface warships to regions of traditional Western naval dominance (for example, the Mediterranean) seems to have reduced the political and diplomatic impact of U.S. naval forces deployed there. Moreover, while only 20 major surface warships have been equipped with such weapons, 66 submarines and 300 naval aircraft are also equipped with cruise missiles. These submarines and aircraft, particularly, implicitly threaten to impose a high cost on any Western decision to intervene with naval forces in regions where Soviet forces can be concentrated. Whether such a threat materializes, however, would depend on the USSR's perceptions of the stakes involved, of its chances in the tactical situation as it was unfolding, of the United States' determination and perception of the situation, and of the overall strategic balance between the superpowers.

In discussing Soviet warship and submarine launched cruise missiles, one must be careful to distinguish between two types. First and second generation

15. *Statement of Admiral Thomas H. Moorer on Department of Defense Appropriations FY 1973,* Hearings before the Senate Appropriations Committee, 92 Cong. 2 sess. (1972), Pt. 1, p. 542. Also see *Statement of Secretary of Defense Melvin R. Laird on Department of Defense Appropriations FY 1973,* ibid., p. 70.

missiles (SS-N-1 and SS-N-3), currently found on most missile-equipped vessels, are of subsonic or transonic speed, surface-launched, and long-range. The latter characteristic usually requires that the missile receive a mid-course correction from some external source, say, a reconnaissance aircraft, if it is to strike its target. All these characteristics make these weapon systems somewhat easier to deal with than the missiles that are superseding them. Submarines of the C class (eight units in 1972), for example, are fitted with the SS-N-7 missile, which is of horizon-range and capable of underwater launch. Additionally, Kresta II-class cruisers and Krivak-class destroyers (a total of four units in 1972) are fitted with the SS-N-10 missile, also a horizon-range weapon and therefore more difficult to counter, except by striking the launch platform preemptively.[16]

Peacetime Deployments

The United States' recently heightened awareness of the Soviet Navy should also be traced to the expanded geographic scope of Soviet naval operations and to the establishment of a continuous Soviet naval presence in several regions of the globe. This trend has developed within the past fifteen years and has been particularly strong since 1967.

The trend has been marked, for example, by a sharp increase in the number of port calls by Soviet vessels in various areas. Soviet naval visits outside the Black and Baltic Seas were most infrequent until 1957.[17] Similarly, the USSR has extended the areas in which it carries out naval exercises. Until 1956, naval maneuvers were held only within the Black, Baltic, and Barents Seas. In the Atlantic, exercise areas were extended slowly through the Norwegian Sea and into the North Atlantic over a period of twelve years. In 1970, the Soviet Union held its first naval exercise of global dimensions—"Okean."[18]

The increase in "out-of-area" operations can best be seen in Soviet deployments to the Mediterranean Sea and the Indian Ocean (Table 4).

A continuous Soviet surface warship presence in the Mediterranean did not begin until after 1964 and did not grow significantly until mid-1967. Total

16. *Jane's Fighting Ships, 1972-73,* p. 577; R. T. Pretty and D. H. R. Archer, *Jane's Weapon Systems, 1971-72* (Jane's Yearbooks, 1971), pp. 43-47.
17. Prominent exceptions were two visits to Britain—one in 1953 in connection with the Spithead Coronation naval review, one in 1955 in connection with Khrushchev's visit to England—and a 1955 visit to China.
18. See MccGwire, "Soviet Naval Capabilities," pp. E6853-55; also Admiral Ephraim P. Holmes, "The Soviet Presence in the Atlantic," *NATO Letter,* Vol. 18 (September 1970), pp. 6-11.

Table 4. Soviet Ship-Operating Days in the Mediterranean Sea and Indian Ocean, 1965-72

Year	Mediterranean Sea[a]	Indian Ocean[b]
1965	4,000	c
1966	4,500	c
1967	8,500	c
1968	12,000	1,800
1969	14,000	2,800
1970	17,500	3,200
1971	19,000	3,400
1972	18,000	8,800

Sources: Data for 1965-71 estimated from a chart appearing in *Statement by Admiral E. R. Zumwalt, Jr. on Fiscal Year 1973 Authorization for Military Procurement,* Hearings before the Senate Committee on Armed Services, 92 Cong. 2 sess. (1972), Pt. 2, p. 923. Data for 1972 from unpublished U.S. Navy sources.
a. Rounded to nearest 500.
b. Rounded to nearest 200.
c. Indicates a total of less than 100.

Soviet ship-operating days in the Mediterranean doubled between 1965 and 1967, doubled once again by 1970, but now seem to have leveled off.

The Soviet buildup in the Mediterranean is also reflected in the annual number of Soviet vessels passing through the Turkish Straits between the Black and Mediterranean Seas. As Figure 1 shows, the number has been sharply rising since 1964 when crossings totaled ninety-four. In 1970, 269 ships passed through the Straits. (These data do not, of course, take into account the fact that some Soviet surface vessels and almost all their submarines enter and leave the Mediterranean through the Straits of Gibraltar, rather than the Bosporus.) The secondary peak in 1960 reflects passage of tankers and other auxiliary vessels supporting the temporary (1958-61) submarine base in Albania.[19]

Soviet combatant units began to deploy to the Indian Ocean regularly in 1968. This presence grew rapidly for two years but then leveled off until 1972. The sharp increase in the past year reflects deployments made in connection with the December 1971 Indo-Pakistani war and to a greater extent the activity of auxiliary vessels engaged in port-clearing operations in Bangladesh. The data in Table 4 include noncombatants (hydrographic research vessels, for instance) as well as warships. Typically, only one-third to one-half of the deployed force consists of warships and submarines.[20]

19. A good discussion of the development of the Soviet Mediterranean deployment is found in Robert G. Weinland, *Soviet Transits of the Turkish Straits,* Professional Paper 94 (Arlington, Va.: Center for Naval Analyses, 1972).
20. *Department of Defense Appropriations for 1973,* Hearings before a subcommittee of the House Committee on Appropriations, 92 Cong. 2 sess. (1972), Pt. 3, pp. 355-56.

Figure 1. Number of Passages of Soviet Naval Vessels through the Turkish Straits, 1945-70

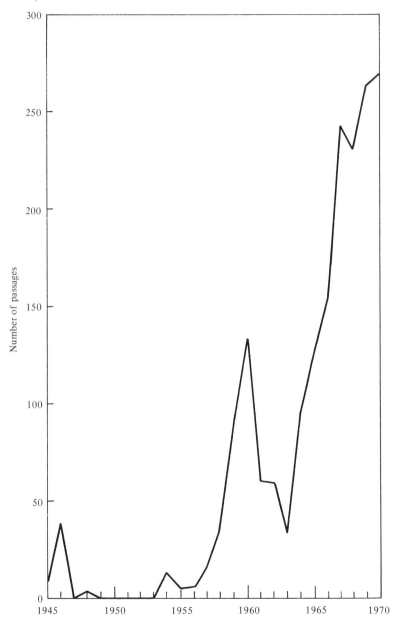

Source: République Turque, Ministre des Affaires Etrangères, "Rapport Annuel sur le Mouvement des Navires à travers les Détroits Turcs" (Ankara, 1946-70; processed).

Elsewhere, surface-warship sorties into the Pacific did not originate until 1963-64 and, into the Caribbean, until 1969. An even more recent development has been the initiation of a nearly continuous but very small presence in the South Atlantic off the West African coast in late 1970.[21]

Given the above data on Soviet Navy force levels, it is clear that the growth in its out-of-area operations is not due to a sudden availability of naval resources. Rather, this trend must reflect a conscious decision by Soviet leaders to expand their peacetime naval presence in foreign waters. Accordingly, it seems likely that either the Soviet Union's perception of requirements for satisfactory performance of its navy's traditional missions has changed or new missions have been assigned to the fleet.

Missions of the Soviet Navy

Naval vessels generally are multifunctional; potentially each may be used to accomplish an assortment of missions. To exploit such possibilities, however, a variety of tasks must be undertaken: suitable equipment procured, tactics developed, personnel trained, deployments made, and various procedures rehearsed. It is possible to infer from observing these preparations the relative importance a navy attaches to each of several potential missions. Such inferences, in turn, provide evidence of a potential opponent's current intentions about the use of naval power. Although intentions are not an infallible guide to the future—naval power developed for one purpose may, in time of conflict, be diverted to other uses—they do constrain a navy's flexibility in various ways. Thus, inferences about Soviet intentions, as evidenced by the sorts of preparations mentioned above and by the composition of the Soviet fleets, and how that has changed over time, can help structure a prudent response to the evolution of Soviet naval capabilities.

In this regard, it is clear that the Soviet Navy has concentrated on the accomplishment of some tasks and largely neglected others. This section reviews the actual and potential missions of the Soviet Navy with a view toward illuminating the relative priorities accorded each by Soviet planners. The missions discussed include strategic offense and defense, political missions, interdiction of shipping, projection of land and air power overseas, and sustained combat at sea.

The reader should be aware that several of these appraisals are controversial. In such cases, alternative points of view are presented.

21. Robert G. Weinland, *The Changing Mission Structure of the Soviet Navy,* Professional Paper 80 (Arlington, Va.: Center for Naval Analyses, 1971), pp. 11-12.

Strategic Defense

Most observers agree that the primary mission of the Soviet Navy is to deter and, if necessary, to blunt any attack on the Soviet homeland from sea-based weapon systems. Two major tasks are involved in strategic defense, each requiring quite distinct types of naval forces.

First, the USSR must maintain the capability to engage and prevent the launch of aircraft from U.S. attack carriers operating in regions within strike range of Soviet territory—particularly, the Eastern Mediterranean and the Norwegian Sea. A substantial increase in the range of U.S. carrier-based strike aircraft in the mid-1950s is said to have prompted Soviet naval procurement decisions made in 1957-58 and to have been the original impetus for extensions in the Soviet Navy's operating areas.[22]

Soviet naval doctrine stresses coordinated operations involving a variety of platforms carrying nuclear-armed missiles for the anticarrier mission, and a very large portion of the Soviet Navy seems to be directed toward this end. As has been noted, a growing portion of the Soviet submarine force is equipped with cruise missiles; in 1972 there were 66 such boats, of the E, J, W-conversion, and C classes. It has been noted also that the newest system, the C class carrying the SS-N-7 missile, provides a qualitatively different order of threat to surface vessels.

In addition, Soviet naval aviation includes about 300 medium-range strike aircraft carrying the AS-2 and AS-5 missiles, designed primarily for anticarrier operations. Also, a "significant portion" of the USSR's "Long Range Aviation" (the equivalent of the United States' Strategic Air Command) is assigned to naval targets.[23] Finally, missile-equipped major surface warships are also assigned anticarrier missions in regions within strike range of the Soviet homeland.

While one would expect the anticarrier mission to have become somewhat less important because of development of the threat from U.S. ballistic missile submarines, defense against carriers retains a prominent position in Soviet naval planning which, like Soviet military planning generally, is characterized by a high degree of conservatism. Anticarrier operations are accorded a central role in all major Soviet naval exercises, including the highly publicized exercise "Okean." In his introduction to a Russian-language book describing "Okean," Defense Minister Grechko noted:

22. MccGwire, in "Soviet Naval Capabilities," provides the best arguments along these lines; a counterposition is provided by Weinland, *The Changing Mission Structure.*

23. Zumwalt letter of June 2, p. 2. In a recent speech, Defense Minister A. A. Grechko indicated that the Strategic Rocket Force also allocated some of its resources to "naval groupings" at sea. *Krasnaya Zvezda* (Dec. 17, 1972), pp. 1-2, translated in Foreign Broadcast Information Service, *Daily Report: Soviet Union* (Dec. 21, 1972), pp. M1-6.

Today aggressive blocs are dominated by imperialist states with large naval forces at their command. These forces are built around groups of fleet ballistic missile submarines (nuclear propulsion) *and attack aircraft carriers with aircraft armed with nuclear weapons. . . .* [The Okean maneuvers] demonstrated to the entire world . . . *our fleet's preparedness to repel any aggression against our country from the sea* and inflict decisive blows on the enemy.[24]

The *second* and more difficult task of strategic defense involves the detection and engagement of deployed Polaris/Poseidon ballistic missile submarines. While there is no evidence suggesting that the Soviet Union has obtained such a capability, it does seem clear that the development of some types of vessels and aircraft has been motivated primarily by a desire to do *something* about the threat posed by strategic submarines. Decisions regarding naval procurement reached during 1961-62 are particularly important in this regard. These forces are unlikely to be effective, however, unless solutions to certain inherent problems are found and unless more capable sensors and weapons are developed.

The anti-strategic-submarine mission generally involves two broad approaches, each of which requires different types of platforms, weapons, and detection systems.

One approach, area defense, focuses on systems capable of detecting submarines over large ocean areas, identifying those that are detected, and sinking them when ordered to do so. The deployment of two antisubmarine helicopter cruisers, the Moskva class, has been a step in this direction, although the area they are capable of searching is still relatively small. More important, deployment of land-based patrol aircraft, IL-38 (May), also could be designed for these purposes. Thirty May aircraft were said to be operational in 1972, and some reportedly were based in Egypt.[25]

The second approach attempts to maintain a continual track on strategic submarines throughout their patrol. In this tactic, a hunter/killer submarine would attach itself to a strategic submarine as the latter left its base or while it was crossing a narrow strait on the way to its patrol area. Using passive sonars, the pursuer would then trail the quarry throughout the latter's period on station. Such a pursuer, if successful, would be in a position to attack the strategic submarine quickly if ordered to do so or should a conflict erupt.

The new Victor-class nuclear attack submarine could be used in this sort of role, but the even newer Alpha class, which has not entered serial production as yet, is a more likely candidate. This is due to the time lag between decision and deployment previously mentioned. At the time the decision to develop

24. N. I. Shablikov and others, *Okean, Maneuvers of the USSR Navy Conducted in April-May 1970,* translated by the Joint Publications Research Service, U.S. Department of Commerce (April 19, 1971; processed), p. 6. (Emphasis added.)

25. *Jane's Fighting Ships, 1972-73,* p. 577; *International Defense Review,* Vol. 5 (October 1972), p. 451.

the Victor must have been made, it is unlikely that the magnitude of the threat posed by U.S. strategic submarines could have been foreseen.

Each of these approaches is plagued by severe problems. Strategic anti-submarine warfare is inherently difficult in that if it is to be performed successfully a large portion of the deployed ballistic missile submarines must be destroyed nearly simultaneously. Otherwise, surviving submarines could be forewarned and would, no doubt, fire their missiles. The damage sustained by receipt of even one submarine-load of missiles would be severe.

The area defense approach bears the particular problem of maintaining contact with a number of submarines in a large area, when the targets' one purpose is to avoid being detected. Indicators of a submarine's presence (for example, noise radiation) are much more emphatic when the submarine is moving at a high rate of speed, such as in the conventional antisubmarine warfare problem, when the target submarine's purpose is to attack merchant ships or other moving surface vessels.

The Russians have expressed some preference for submarine-based anti-submarine warfare—the second approach.[26] There are also problems in this approach, however. First, countermeasures are available to the quarry when it is leaving port, the point when it is most susceptible to initial detection. For example, the quarry can exit close to merchant ships, using their radiated noise to mask its own trail, or it can be assisted by surface naval forces in eluding possible pursuers. If the strategic submarine discovers a pursuer during its patrol, it can take various evasive actions or deploy noise-making devices as decoys. Moreover, if it were discovered that one or the other side's strategic submarines were being trailed by the opponent, this would be likely to have serious consequences for the general state of relations between the United States and the Soviet Union. Since ballistic missile submarines are viewed as the keystone of each superpower's strategic deterrent, the existence of such trails could raise fears that the pursuer's nation was preparing for a first strike, and thus would be destabilizing to the strategic relationship.[27]

Strategic Offense

A major feature of the evolution of Soviet naval capabilities since 1958 has been the appearance of a credible, sea-based strategic missile force. The con-

26. For example, N. I. Suzdalev, *Podvodnye lodki protiv podvodnykh lodok* (Submarines against Submarines) (Moscow: Military Publishing House, 1968).

27. For a discussion of problems and prospects in strategic ASW, see Richard Garwin, "Anti-Submarine Warfare and National Security," *Scientific American*, Vol. 227 (July 1972), pp. 14-25.

struction rate of strategic submarines in recent years alone, nine to ten a year, indicates the high priority accorded this mission by Soviet planners. Consequently, most observers also credit it as being of primary importance. The Yankee-class submarine, equipped with sixteen SS-N-6 missiles, is the first Soviet sea-based strategic weapon system worthy of serious concern in the West. Moreover, a longer-range sea-based missile (SS-N-8) has been tested and will be deployed, twelve per boat, in a modified version of the Yankee, known as the Delta class.[28]

Under the terms of the arms limitation agreement signed in May 1972, the Soviet Union is permitted to deploy 740 ballistic missile launchers at sea, plus an additional 210 launchers provided it retires an equal number of older land-based missile systems.[29] This will give the Russians an edge in number of launchers over the United States, and a force of 46 to 62 strategic submarines depending on the eventual mix of 12- and 16-tube units and whether they avail themselves of the option regarding the replacement of land-based missiles. It can be assumed that the older Soviet ballistic missile submarines—H, G, and Z(V) classes—will be retired in the not too distant future.

In range and perhaps accuracy, the Soviet Yankee/SS-N-6 system is roughly equivalent to the Polaris/A-1 system fully deployed by the United States in the mid-1960s. The SS-N-8 missile is more like later U.S. weapons, though not like the United States' most modern systems.[30] In two important respects the Soviet sea-based strategic missile force remains markedly inferior to the U.S. force: (a) the Soviet Union has not yet developed the technology necessary to deploy multiple independently targetable reentry vehicles (MIRVs), such as the U.S. Poseidon system, and it is unlikely to do so for several years; (b) U.S. submarines are quieter and consequently less susceptible to detection than their Soviet counterparts.[31]

28. *Washington Post,* May 13, 1971. The first modified Yankee may be already operational; see *New York Times,* Oct. 1, 1972, and *Washington Star,* Feb. 6, 1973.

29. *Protocol—to the Interim Agreement Between the United States of America and the Union of Soviet Socialist Republics on Certain Measures with Respect to the Limitation of Strategic Offensive Arms,* May 26, 1972; reprinted in *Military Implications of the Treaty on the Limitation of Anti-Ballistic Missile Systems, and the Interim Agreement on Limitation of Strategic Offensive Arms,* Hearings before the Senate Committee on Armed Services, 92 Cong. 2 sess. (1972), p. 15.

30. The Soviet Union seems to have exceeded U.S. capabilities in one respect—range. Secretary Laird reported that the most recent flight test of the SS-N-8 was about 4,000 nautical miles. *Aviation Week and Space Technology,* Vol. 97 (Dec. 4, 1972), p. 5.

31. See "Interview with Defense Secretary Laird," *U.S. News and World Report* (March 27, 1972), p. 44; and letter from Admiral E. R. Zumwalt, Jr., to Senator William Proxmire, June 8, 1972, p. 5; reprinted in *Congressional Record* (June 12, 1972), pp. S9193-95. (Cited hereafter as Zumwalt letter of June 8.)

Given these differences, the Soviet sea-based strategic system deployed in the early to mid-1980s is likely to be qualitatively comparable to the U.S. Poseidon fleet due to be deployed completely by 1976. Narrowing this technological gap will no doubt remain an important goal in Soviet plans and policies. Even in the absence of such a narrowing, however, strategic submarines are an important element in the Soviet deterrent posture and would pose a serious threat to the United States should deterrence fail.

Missions Supporting Foreign Policy Objectives

Naval vessels can be used to further the foreign policy goals of their owners in a manner only indirectly related to the war-fighting capabilities of the ships. The movement of warships, their activity while on patrol, and their ports of call can be used to signal a state's intentions in various situations—as a means of commitment, as a threat, and so forth. In addition, naval forces can perform various acts which, while certainly hostile, incorporate only limited and measured degrees of force; blockade and interposition fall into this category. In each of these situations, naval activity is designed to have an impact on the expectations of the nations directly involved and on those that might consider becoming involved. Such naval activity is generally accompanied by diplomatic or other forms of verbal behavior, and serves as a signal of the seriousness with which these verbal communications should be understood. The traditional maritime nations have long employed naval forces for such purposes in a form of behavior widely referred to as "gunboat diplomacy."

The mere presence of a naval force in a region serves a political function, regardless of its composition, its missions, or its activity, and even in the absence of any diplomatic activity directed toward similar ends. The existence of the force automatically causes the states of the region to weigh a new factor in their calculations of the balance of power and in their expectations of the probable behavior of other states in various contingencies. As such, a state that establishes a peacetime naval presence in a specific region is apt to gain influence in the affairs of that region.

At the extreme and in the long run, some believe that such phenomena could contribute to the possible realignment of international allegiances. This thought might be of particular relevance in periods when some observers seem to perceive the relative preponderance of naval power to be shifting from one state to another. These perceptions may or may not reflect accurately the objective reality of the naval balance.

The potential political consequences of naval activity become more apparent during international crises. During periods of international tensions, naval powers traditionally have used their maritime resources to signal their intentions, to bluff, to commit themselves to certain actions, to force the opponent to risk a major conflict if he wishes to intervene in the situation, to signal the termination of the crisis, and so forth. Naval forces in a region can be reinforced; they can be moved closer to or farther from the trouble spot; they can be interposed between the opponent's forces and the source of tension; they can harass the opposing forces or act in a provocative and threatening manner; and they can provide various forms of combat capability. Again, however, the impact of navies in these situations is likely to be less a function of the actual military characteristics of the forces themselves than of their symbolic value. Their effectiveness will depend on the credibility possible adversaries attribute to the threatening behavior and the extent to which they value the stakes involved in the local conflict relative to the stakes involved in the overall relations between the great powers.[32]

There is some controversy over the importance of these politically oriented missions for the Soviet Navy and the degree to which a desire to have such capabilities may have affected their shipbuilding programs. Some observers trace adoption of political and diplomatic roles by the Soviet Navy to the Cuban missile crisis. The United States' ability to challenge the Soviet Union at sea, to blockade Cuba, and to credibly threaten an invasion is said to have demonstrated to the USSR the value of naval forces for such purposes and to have caused it to resolve never to be placed in such a position of military inferiority again. Most significant, the Cuban missile crisis is said to have convinced the Soviet Union that strategic nuclear power was not a sufficient basis for attainment of its foreign policy goals, that it also would be necessary to develop general purpose forces capable of defending its foreign interests. Consequently, this viewpoint traces much of the subsequent evolution of Soviet naval capabilities, particularly the development of new surface warships, to this event.[33]

Many of those holding this view pay particular attention to traditional Russian interests in the Middle East. It is argued that a strong motivation for the Soviet Union to augment its naval capabilities has been a desire to project Soviet power, in a political sense, into the Eastern Mediterranean—a region

32. For an interesting discussion of the political utility of naval forces of the great powers in the 1971 Indo-Pakistani war, see James M. McConnell and Anne M. Kelly, *Superpower Naval Diplomacy in the Indo-Pakistani Crisis,* Professional Paper (Arlington, Va.: Center for Naval Analyses, 1973).

33. Lt. Cdr. David R. Cox, "Seapower and Soviet Foreign Policy," *U.S. Naval Institute Proceedings,* Vol. 95 (June 1969), pp. 35-36; Col. Thomas W. Wolfe, *The Soviet Quest for More Globally Mobile Military Power,* Memo RM-5554-PR (Santa Monica: RAND Corp., 1967); *Statement by Admiral E. R. Zumwalt, Jr. on Fiscal Year 1973 Authorization for Military Procurement,* Hearings before the Senate Committee on Armed Services, 92 Cong. 2 sess. (1972), Pt. 2, pp. 915-16.

which the USSR may well regard much as the United States views the Caribbean. This motivation may have been reinforced by the sharp political impact of the Soviet Union's early and quite modest excursions into the region, leading to renewed efforts to augment the size and capabilities of the Soviet Mediterranean squadron.

Other observers, however, downplay the significance of political purposes in general and of the missile crisis in particular as motives for Soviet naval expansion. They point out that, long before 1962, the Soviet and even Tsarist navies had on occasion undertaken political missions. Furthermore, the necessarily long lead times between decisions and new ship deployments indicate that development of the new classes of warships that made their initial appearance in the late 1960s was probably instituted before the missile crisis. This viewpoint sees the structure of the Soviet Navy as being primarily a function of Soviet perceptions of the requirements for strategic defense.[34] Most observers would agree, in any case, that present deployment patterns can be attributed partially to political missions.[35]

Regardless of this debate, the Soviet Navy has in recent years been used in various ways for political and diplomatic purposes. In addition to the general political impact of the establishment of a Soviet naval presence in various regions, four specific types of political roles may be illustrated.

First, the USSR has employed its navy to try to constrain the U.S. role in crises in the Middle East, Africa, and South Asia. This mission is frequently cited by Soviet leaders as justification for their presence in the Mediterranean. For example, at a time of considerable tension in the Mediterranean, Admiral Gorshkov, the Soviet Commander-in-Chief, said:

Ships of the Soviet Navy are systematically present in the ocean, including the areas of the presence of shock navies [naval strike forces-BB] of NATO. The presence of our ships in these areas binds the hands of the imperialists, deprives them of a possibility to interfere unhindered into internal affairs of the peoples.[36]

There have been reports indicating that unusually large numbers of Soviet combatant vessels were maintained in the general area of the fighting during the 1967 Arab-Israeli war, the 1970 Jordanian civil war, and the 1971 Indo-

34. For arguments on this subject see Michael MccGwire, "Soviet Maritime Strategy, Capabilities, and Intentions in the Caribbean," in J. D. Theberge (ed.), *Soviet Seapower in the Caribbean* (Praeger, 1972), pp. 39-54.

35. Weinland, *The Changing Mission Structure.*

36. Tass, International Service, July 25, 1970, reprinted in Foreign Broadcast Information Service, *Daily Report: Soviet Union* (July 27, 1971), p. E-1.

Pakistani war.[37] Presumably, these deployments were made in response to (or in anticipation of) U.S. activity with the purpose of deterring the unilateral exercise of Western naval power, such as was the case during the Lebanese crisis in 1958.

Soviet naval spokesmen have claimed considerable success in the performance of this mission and are fond of pointing out the difference between present conditions and those of the not too distant past. For example, in another statement Admiral Gorshkov said:

> Due to the presence in seas and oceans of the Soviet Navy, Healey, the former English minister of war, was forced to admit that "as a result of the presence of Soviet naval forces, the countries of the West will not easily decide to intervene as they did at the time of the Lebanese crisis in 1958." Yes, the situation has changed, and not to the advantage of the imperialists. They are now forced to seriously take into account the presence of Soviet ships in the Mediterranean.[38]

Whether the United States and its allies were actually constrained may be less important than whether other nations believed them to have been so hampered. For example, Radio Tripoli claimed that Soviet naval operations deterred British intervention following the coup d'etat in Libya in 1969.[39] In point of fact, Britain and the United States controlled air bases in Libya at the time and would not necessarily have had to intervene by sea even if the Soviet Union had interposed a force. Moreover, the Soviet Union itself has not claimed credit for this "defeat" of the imperialists.

Second, the Soviet Navy has been used in situations not involving the United States, in actions designed to protect Soviet client states or other governments from threats mounted by their enemies, domestic and foreign. Increasing Soviet involvement in the Third World implies greater Soviet commitments to such governments. On occasion, the USSR has used its naval resources to demonstrate and implement those commitments. For example, in the fall of 1967, Soviet warships visited Port Said following the sinking of the *Eilat* in an obvious attempt to deter Israeli reprisals.[40] In the spring of 1970, prolonged port calls were made to Mogadishu, Somali Republic, seemingly as a means of demonstrating support for the incumbent regime threatened

37. *New York Times,* May 31, 1967, and Oct. 8, 1970; *Philadelphia Inquirer,* Dec. 17, 1971; Zumwalt, *Statement on FY 1973 Authorization for Military Procurement,* p. 5; and McConnell and Kelly, *Superpower Naval Diplomacy.*

38. *Pravda,* July 30, 1972, reprinted in Foreign Broadcast Information Service, *Daily Report: Soviet Union* (Aug. 1, 1972), p. M-7.

39. Reported in James Cable, *Gunboat Diplomacy* (Praeger, 1971), pp. 146-47.

40. Cox, "Seapower and Soviet Foreign Policy," pp. 42-43.

by domestic instability.[41] In December 1970, Soviet units established a naval patrol off the coast of Guinea, apparently to deter further Portuguese incursions, such as had been staged the previous month.[42]

Third, on at least one occasion the USSR seems to have used naval vessels to coerce another nation, in defense of Soviet maritime resources. In the best example to date of Soviet recourse to traditional gunboat diplomacy, warships were deployed off the coast of Ghana in February-March 1969 in conjunction with diplomatic efforts to secure the release of Soviet fishing trawlers. The fishing boats had been impounded the previous October because of their alleged involvement in arms smuggling. Following the failure of diplomatic and economic activity to secure their release, the Soviet Union in an unprecedented move deployed three warships to the Gulf of Guinea. Their presence off the Ghanaian coast coincided with release of the trawlers.[43]

Finally, ships of the Soviet Navy have made increasing use of local port facilities in recent years. While most port visits are primarily designed to meet operational requirements generated by the maintenance of a permanent naval presence in distant waters, they also can be used to create goodwill between the host nation and the Soviet Union. Moreover, certain situations lend themselves to the use of port visits for more immediate and direct political ends. For example, in May 1971 Soviet warship visits to Sierra Leone seem to have been used to help legitimize a new and shaky regime.[44]

Projection of Land and Air Power Overseas

To a certain extent, the effectiveness of a navy in political roles will be dependent on its projection capability—the physical capacity of that military force to intervene in situations overseas with men, equipment, or air power. In any event, this capability has important military implications.

Forces primarily designed to accomplish the projection mission have consumed the major portion of the U.S. Navy's budget during the past decade. Perhaps for this reason, American commentators have tended to stress potential Soviet interest in similar pursuits. Much has been made of the USSR's reactivation of naval infantry (that is, marines) in 1963 and of the assumed potential of Moskva-class helicopter cruisers to serve as assault ships or to

41. James M. McConnell, *The Soviet Navy in the Indian Ocean,* Professional Paper 77 (Arlington, Va.: Center for Naval Analyses, 1971), p. 11.
42. Weinland, *The Changing Mission Structure,* p. 11; *Washington Post,* Feb. 9, 1972.
43. Weinland, *The Changing Mission Structure,* p. 11.
44. Ibid., p. 12.

accommodate vertical or short takeoff and landing (V/STOL) aircraft.[45]

At present, however, the projection capability of the Soviet Navy is modest. For one thing, the Soviet Union's naval infantry is reported to consist of only 15,000 men. For another, the newest and largest ship in the Soviet amphibious force, the Alligator class, displaces only 4,000 tons and resembles a large landing ship (tank), one of the smaller U.S. vessels used for such purposes. It can carry only 1,700 tons of material and deliver it over the beach by landing craft. The USSR has also deployed several classes of even smaller amphibious vessels since 1958. It is doubtful, however, if the unloaded displacement of the Soviet Union's entire amphibious force (some 100 vessels excluding landing craft) exceeds 125,000 tons. Furthermore, the USSR has not deployed any amphibious warfare ships designed for helicopter assault operations.

For comparison, in the past few years the United States has initiated construction of five amphibious assault ships (LHA). Each ship displaces 40,000 tons and can carry a reinforced battalion of Marines (1,825 men). Also, since 1960 the United States has deployed seven LPHs (Iwo Jima class), fifteen LPDs (Austin and Raleigh classes), five LSDs (Anchorage class), and twenty LSTs (Newport class). All these ships, except the LSTs, are capable of helicopter operations. In total, the post-1960 U.S. force can carry nearly 130,000 troops and will displace (unloaded) some 700,000 tons. Thus the total Soviet amphibious force is only one-fifth the size of the portion of its U.S. counterpart built since 1960 alone. But the differing geographic scope of Soviet and U.S. interests makes this comparison of limited value. The warning at the beginning of this paper against taking such comparisons too seriously is relevant here.

More important is the lack of evidence that either the *Moskva* or its sister helicopter cruiser has been used in other than antisubmarine operations. In addition, the Soviet Navy currently has no capability to deploy fixed-wing aircraft on naval vessels and thus could neither supply air cover for an amphibious landing nor provide sea-based air power to client regimes.[46]

---

45. For example, see J. T. Howes, *Multicrises: Seapower and Global Politics in the Missile Age* (M.I.T. Press, 1971), pp. 305-07.

46. It should be mentioned that the Soviet Union has other resources that could be used to compensate for some of these deficiencies. For example, air cover could be flown in or transported by merchant shipping, as the Soviet Union demonstrated in Egypt in 1969, so long as the seas and air space remained sanctuaries. Similarly, the USSR could use its merchant shipping fleet to transport several combat divisions. Such capabilities, however, are quite different from those necessary to undertake operations in wartime, and are not as flexible or as quickly reactive as true sea-based interventionary forces would be. Moreover, the important thing is that the Soviet decision not to develop forces designed solely for amphibious assault or sea-based air power demonstrates the relatively low priority which the USSR assigns to these missions.

Under such conditions, it seems likely that the only projection missions envisioned by Soviet planners at present are: (a) those that can be undertaken under peacetime conditions, as was the case in Egypt in 1969; and (b) those in regions contiguous to the Soviet Union and within range of Soviet land-based aircraft. The latter is generally thought of as means of the Soviet fleets' securing access to and from their confined home waters during a more general conflict.[47] Of greatest priority in this regard would be seizure of the Turkish Straits; of secondary priority, seizure of the northern coast of Norway and the Baltic approaches. Given the importance of these regions to the defense of NATO, however, it would be imprudent to discount completely Soviet amphibious capabilities. The final section of this paper will discuss the possible expansion of Soviet projection capabilities in the future.

Interdiction of Sea Lanes of Communication

Potential missions of the Soviet Navy which are usually referred to as "interdiction" include two separable contingencies. One foresees the possibility of a major conflict in Europe or elsewhere and the use of Soviet submarines and naval aviation to disrupt U.S. efforts to deploy and supply military forces in the combat theater. The other contingency, which has been termed "commerce war of attrition," considers the possibility of submarine and air interdiction of civilian merchant shipping, either in conjunction with a protracted land war or independently as a form of limited war. Recently the possibility has been raised that the commerce war of attrition might focus on U.S. and allied oil imports from the Persian Gulf.[48] The importance of these missions to the Soviet Navy and the degree to which they might influence Soviet naval planning are points on which Western analysts disagree, particularly on commerce wars of attrition.

Some U.S. Navy spokesmen have emphasized these missions as a primary purpose of Soviet naval development. For example, in 1971 Admiral Zumwalt stated:

The new Soviet Navy with its main power in weapons designed for interdiction—submarines and anti-ship missiles launched from Long Range Aviation, Naval Aviation, surface and submarine platforms—have been designed to counter our naval forces and deny us the use of the seas to support our allied and our overseas forces. Once isolated, the U.S. would be denied a forward defense posture and our allies would be forced to seek accommodations with the

47. MccGwire, "Soviet Naval Capabilities," p. E6854.
48. Zumwalt, Statement on FY 1973 Authorization for Military Procurement, p. 3.

Soviets or the CPR. The mere sufficient evidence in peacetime of Soviet capability to do this would be enough to start the erosion of our alliances and lay the basis for accommodations by our allies with the USSR.[49]

This viewpoint is based on two major premises.

First, it is undeniable that the sea lanes of communication are of major importance to the Western alliance. They are essential to trade in peacetime and important to the economic well-being of the nations involved. Also in peacetime, they are essential for the importation of some basic commodities, petroleum being a case in point. The sea lanes are important in wartime since the largest share of military supplies are always moved by sea. This has been demonstrated on several occasions, the war in Vietnam being the latest example. Moreover, the Soviet Union observed the significant damage imposed on Western shipping by the Germans in World War II. Because of the importance of the sea lanes, and because of the difficulty of defending surface shipping from submarine attack, it seems logical to assume that the Soviet Union would recognize and seek to exploit this potential vulnerability.

Second, those who believe that interdiction is of major importance to the Soviet Union stress the large number of torpedo attack and cruise missile submarines they have deployed. It is noted in particular that one-third of these are assigned to the Northern Fleet, which is responsible for the Atlantic area.[50] Advocates of this viewpoint question whether the Soviet Union would have built as many submarines as it did if it did not intend to use them for interdiction. Similar questions are sometimes directed at the relatively large number of medium-range strike aircraft assigned to Soviet Naval Aviation.

The opposite position—that interdiction missions are of limited importance in Soviet naval planning—stems partly from the view that such a priority would be anomalous in the face of Soviet emphasis on short wars, as evidenced by Soviet military doctrine and by the composition and structure of Soviet ground forces. In a short war, military and civilian resupply would be of much lesser importance than in a protracted conflict. If the Soviet Union plans its ground forces on the assumption that conflicts will be of limited duration, it seems unlikely that it would design its naval forces for longer wars.

49. *Military Posture and H.R. 3818 and H.R. 8687,* Hearings before the House Committee on Armed Services, 92 Cong. 1 sess. (1971), Pt. 1, p. 2762.

50. Estimates of the distribution of Soviet naval forces can be found in Breyer, *Guide to the Soviet Navy,* pp. 3-10; and in a paper by Robert Berman in MccGwire (ed.), "Soviet Naval Development," pp. 113-17.

Many students of Soviet affairs[51] have argued that the USSR makes little or no provision for protracted warfare in Europe, and that its armies are designed, equipped, and deployed so as to win "a short war based on shock power."[52] These arguments pay particular attention to the relative weakness of the Soviet Union's logistical system, its relatively high ratio of combat to support troops, its use of a unit rather than an individual personnel replacement system, and its military writings and exercises.

Those subscribing to these views explain that the large number of torpedo attack and cruise missile submarines and medium-range strike aircraft are the result of Soviet perceptions of the requirements for strategic defense, particularly of those requirements generated by the anticarrier mission. They note that Soviet Naval Aviation is not particularly well suited for the interdiction mission; the range of its aircraft is scarcely great enough to reach Atlantic shipping lanes without overflying European air defenses. In wartime, Western merchant or military convoys could be routed further south and then proceed north along the African and European coasts under the protection of NATO land-based fighter aircraft.

Those subscribing to this view further note that there is no public evidence of Soviet naval maneuvers involving coordinated interdiction campaigns. Soviet naval exercises continue to emphasize anticarrier operations. Finally, they ask why, if the USSR emphasizes interdiction in naval planning, the number of torpedo attack submarines has declined more steeply than any other component of the Soviet Navy during the past fourteen years (from 474 to 225). Even though a portion of this decline may be explained by the increase in individual unit capabilities, and even though cruise missile submarines (66 units in 1972) also could be used for interdiction, it seems that the sharp decline in attack submarine force levels is reflective of the relatively low priority the Soviet Union places on interdiction.

In the writer's opinion, the weight of evidence lies with those who doubt the significance of interdiction missions for Soviet naval planning. That being

51. For example, John Erickson, *Soviet Military Power* (London: Royal United Service Institute, 1971); McConnell, "Ideology and Soviet Military Strategy"; Malcolm MacIntosh, "The Role of Flexible Response in Soviet Strategic Thinking," paper presented at the first "Symposium on Soviet Affairs" (Garmisch-Partenkirchen, Germany, 1967); "The Adaptation of Soviet Ground Forces to Nuclear War" (anonymous), *Military Review,* Vol. 46 (September 1966), pp. 11-17.

52. Steven L. Canby, "NATO Military Policy: The Constraints Imposed by an Inappropriate Military Structure" (1972, processed), p. 15. A modified version of this paper appears as "NATO Muscle: More Shadow Than Substance," *Foreign Policy,* No. 8 (Fall 1972), pp. 38-49.

said, however, it is still necessary to qualify this conclusion. Regardless of its intentions, it is true that the Soviet Union has substantial forces that potentially could be used to interdict Western shipping. It is also true that the West could be vulnerable in this regard. If a protracted war in Europe should develop, an occurrence which is possible regardless of either side's plans and military doctrine, Soviet submarines and strike aircraft which survived engagements resulting from their primary missions—the attack of carriers and other naval task forces—would, no doubt, be used to attack Western military supply and civilian merchant shipping. It has been pointed out, for example, that German doctrine, training, and force levels before both World Wars did not indicate the use of submarines to interdict merchant shipping, a tactic that was used to good advantage once each war began.[53]

The distinction is one between intentions and capabilities. Its implications, if one accepts this writer's view, are as follows:

(a) The requirements for interdiction campaigns do not now play a significant role in Soviet planning or in their present decisions regarding the future direction the Soviet Navy will assume. Also, a commerce war of attrition independent of a major land battle should be considered a most unlikely course of action for the USSR.[54]

(b) Nonetheless, should a major land conflict develop, the Soviet Union would use its available resources in attempts to interdict Western military and civilian shipping and would have a considerable capability in this respect.

Sustained Combat at Sea

The absence of sea-based air power in the Soviet Navy limits the force's ability to maintain surface units at sea in hostile environments. This limitation is further aggravated by three additional factors.

Support forces. It has been noted that the Soviet Union largely has neglected the construction of support forces. While it still has been able to maintain substantial continuous deployments in distant areas, making use of civilian ships and local port facilities for support, such a logistical system presumes a

53. For example, at the outset of World War II Germany had only 57 submarines; this force was rapidly expanded, reaching 400 for a brief period in 1942. See F. H. Hinsley, *Hitler's Strategy* (Toronto: Macmillan, 1951), and Reinhard Scheer, *Germany's High Sea Fleet in the World War* (London: Cassell, 1920). The writer is indebted to Vice-Admiral Stansfield Turner, president of the Naval War College, for pointing out these historical precedents.

54. Persuasive arguments in this regard are presented in Michael MccGwire, "The Submarine Threat to Western Shipping: A Critical Evaluation" (1969; processed).

peacetime environment. In wartime, such arrangements would be considered neither practical nor secure. There are, however, some signs—such as the use of the side-by-side replenishment method[55]—that the Soviet Union will soon upgrade its logistics capabilities afloat.

Ship design. Observers have marveled at the relatively small size of Soviet warships. New Soviet destroyers are roughly only half the size of their American counterparts, for example, yet demonstrate considerable advantage in some areas, such as firepower. While part of this difference may be attributed to greater Soviet advances in ship design, clearly some capabilities have had to be sacrificed to achieve smaller size and its consequent lower cost. These sacrifices—which include crew habitability, range, endurance, and reload capacity[56]—strongly affect their capability for sustained combat at sea.

Overseas bases. The consequences of both the above factors are aggravated by the USSR's reluctance to make use of bases overseas. While of necessity the USSR has made use of certain facilities in Egypt and of facilities in Syria since the Egyptian government's decision to reduce the Soviet presence in July 1972,[57] the development of the Soviet Union's shore establishment has not kept pace with its rapidly growing deployments. Whether for ideological reasons, because of Soviet observation of problems the United States faces connected with its bases, or because of lack of opportunities, the Soviet Navy's support infrastructure in foreign countries is relatively limited. Although much has been made of Soviet arrangements with various states for the use of ports and airfields for the support of merchant, fishing, and in some cases, naval vessels, such arrangements are quite different from the attainment of less transitory and more exclusive naval "bases."[58] The use of foreign facilities is helpful in maintaining a standing peacetime presence in distant areas; such facilities are, however, unlikely to be helpful in conflict situations, or at least Soviet decision makers cannot count on their availability. As the United States has learned from various Mediterranean experiences, even the use of naval "bases" is often restricted by host governments.

55. U.S. and other Western navies replenish with the ships steaming side-by-side. This is the fastest and most efficient method, but requires considerable seamanship. Until recently, Soviet ships were only observed replenishing bow-to-stern—a slower but less difficult process.

56. Zumwalt letters of June 2 and 8.

57. The status of Soviet naval facilities in the Middle East is unclear at present. A recent report indicated that they have lost the use of Egyptian bases for the reconnaissance of the U.S. Sixth Fleet, and no longer have exclusive use of ship facilities at Alexandria and Mersa Matruh. *Christian Science Monitor,* Dec. 16, 1972.

58. In a statement of May 1972 that presaged his expulsion of the Soviet military from Egypt, President Sadat carefully distinguished between "facilities" and "bases." *Radio Cairo Domestic Service,* May 1, 1972.

Because of these three factors, serious questions arise regarding the ability of the Soviet Navy to function on the surface outside areas contiguous to the fleet's home waters except in a peacetime environment or at the very beginning of hostilities. On the other hand, in regions close to the Soviet Union, such as the Barents, Baltic, and Black Seas, the support problem is not as difficult, and Soviet surface warships would be able to operate under the cover of land-based aircraft. Since these are the areas in which the Soviet Union is most likely to want to operate, these exceptions are of considerable importance. In addition, the priority of the sustained surface combat mission may be upgraded in the future, if the USSR develops better logistical systems and sea-based air power, and perhaps feels compelled to acquire a more extensive overseas shore establishment.

Future Directions in Soviet Naval Development

There are some indications that changes in Soviet naval planning may currently be under consideration. The Soviet Navy seems to be approaching a turning point in its evolution. Many programs that were long under development are now completed or have resulted in series production of various types of units. Forces have been deployed that seem to be capable of successfully carrying out certain long sought after missions, although others (such as the anti-strategic-submarine mission) remain far from complete.

The Commander-in-Chief of the Soviet Navy, Admiral S. G. Gorshkov, has been in office almost twenty years and may soon be ready to step down. Speculation about the admiral's possible retirement and about the existence of a new internal Soviet debate on naval force structure and missions has been fueled by publication of a series of monthly articles written by Admiral Gorshkov in the Soviet Navy journal, *Morskoi Sbornik.*[59]

This series, ostensibly a history of the Russian and Soviet navies, appears to be, in fact, a remarkably open discussion of conflicting approaches to the navy's role, couched in historical terms. In these articles the admiral argues for a larger navy, one capable of denying use of important ocean areas to the United States and of exerting positive control over regions contiguous to the USSR. He argues the need for this major naval force, even if it must come at the expense of other components of the Soviet military. In large part, the

---

59. Admiral S. G. Gorshkov, "Navies in War and in Peace," *Morskoi Sbornik* (February 1972-February 1973). I am indebted to Robert W. Herrick for assisting me in understanding these articles. See his article, "The Gorshkov Interpretation of Russian Naval History," in MccGwire (ed.), "Soviet Naval Development," pp. 275-92.

admiral bases his case on the unique value of navies in peacetime–their use to maintain good relations between states, to demonstrate a nation's military and economic might, and to resolve various problems of foreign policy. He reminds the readers of historical examples when the Russians were ill-prepared for conflict because of their neglect of naval forces and blames this on poor understanding of the value of sea power by many Russian leaders. He cleverly notes that "there is widespread propaganda produced by American ideologists asserting that the Soviet state does not need a powerful Navy,"[60] thus placing those who oppose naval expansion in the imperialist camp.

The appearance of these articles, with their openly polemical nature, is quite surprising. As the Soviet system places a high premium on secrecy in policy debates, their appearance seems to indicate an extraordinary occurrence.

One possibility is that Soviet naval construction programs and the maintenance of standing naval forces in relatively distant areas has come under attack. Such an attack would be based on the relatively high cost of these measures and the burden they place on the Soviet economy, particularly in view of the limited tangible benefits derived from them to date (the 1972 withdrawal of Soviet military units from Egypt is a case in point). The attack might have been mounted by influential party leaders primarily concerned with economic affairs, supported by Defense Ministry officials (mainly army officers).

A second possibility is that present Soviet naval plans and deployments have not come under attack, but that Gorshkov is trying to expand both the commonly accepted conception of the navy's role and naval building programs and has met with opposition.

Still a third possibility is that the Soviet Union has already decided to expand the role of its navy, and Gorshkov's articles are designed to defend and justify this decision to lower ranking civilian and military officials.

Basically, the choice facing the Soviet Union is this. It can maintain, more or less, the present size and composition of the navy except for the inevitable reductions in torpedo attack submarines and destroyers mentioned in the first section. If such a choice were made, there would be continued modernization as improved weapons, sensors, and other equipment became available through technological development, but these measures would continue to concentrate on currently emphasized missions–strategic defense and offense and countering the West's naval forces close to Soviet shores.

Alternatively, the Soviet Union could begin to develop the forces necessary to exert positive control of the seas and to project its power more effectively

60. Gorshkov, "Russia's Difficult Road to the Sea," *Morskoi Sbornik,* No. 3 (March 1972), p. 21.

far from its own shores. Prerequisites for such a capability would include: (a) development of new classes of surface warships; (b) acquisition of a sea-based fixed-wing aircraft capability; (c) construction of larger and more capable assault forces; (d) expansion of the navy's land-based infrastructure; and (e) development of logistics forces capable of providing support on the high seas in hostile environments. These measures would be costly and would result in a marked increase in the resources expended by the Soviet Navy. In view of other pressing civilian and military demands upon the Soviet Union's limited resources, this argues against the adoption of such a course of action. Nonetheless, several factors lead one to reserve judgment as to the eventual outcome.

First, the public prominence of the Soviet Navy and its use in various political roles are fairly recent phenomena, 1967 being a good point of reference for the renewed emphasis on such activity. The Soviet Union has enjoyed the prestige accorded it because of this prominence and has reaped specific, if still limited benefits, in India, Somalia, Guinea, and elsewhere. While the 1972 downturn in Soviet fortunes in Egypt will bolster the arguments of those who take the opposing view, these other successes may well spur the Soviet Union to obtain the capabilities necessary to achieve similar outcomes in less marginal situations—even those involving greater risk of conflict with the United States.

Second, in 1972 the first ship of a new class of guided missile cruiser, the *Kara,* made its initial public appearance. One or two other ships of this class were reported to be under construction. The vessel is important as it is considerably larger than other modern Soviet cruisers (9,000 tons versus 6,000 for the Kresta II) and thus is probably intended as a replacement for the larger but older Sverdlov-class gun cruisers, built between 1951 and 1956. The size of the *Kara* should make ships of this class well suited for sustained operations at sea. The added space could be used to improve endurance and reload capacity, and to equip the vessels as flagships with additional communications gear and staff accommodations.[61] The importance of the *Kara* as an indicator of Soviet intentions should not be exaggerated, however, insofar as a replacement for the Sverdlov-class obviously was necessary and because the decision to build the *Kara* was probably made some time ago. Nonetheless, the class is an important improvement in Soviet capabilities for sustained operations on the high seas.

Third, and more significant, are reports of the construction of one and possibly two much larger vessels, expected to be some type of aircraft carrier, in the Nikolaev shipyard on the Black Sea. In the past, Soviet spokesmen have disparaged the efficacy of aircraft carriers. Recently, however, Admiral

61. *Jane's Fighting Ships, 1972-73,* pp. 80, 612; *New York Times,* Oct. 17, 1972.

Zumwalt stated: "We now have evidence that the Soviet Navy . . . is reevaluating its requirements and is planning to take tactical aircraft to sea. We project that the Soviets' first carrier will, in fact, appear within the next few years."[62] Estimates of the new vessel's size have ranged between 25,000 and 45,000 tons. It is said to be capable of aircraft operations, having an angled flight deck roughly 600 feet long.[63]

The significance of the vessel will depend on its actual size, the types of aircraft operating from it, and its function. Current size estimates may be exaggerated somewhat, since U.S. intelligence forecasts are, understandably, likely to be prudently biased on the high side. Initial public estimates of the size of the *Moskva*, which did not appear until after the ship had begun its sea trials (a point still more than a year away for the new ship), overestimated that vessel's size by more than 25 percent.[64]

It appears unlikely that the new ship will be used to operate modern fixed-wing jet aircraft. It is much smaller than newer U.S. carriers used for this purpose (60,000 to 95,000 tons). Nor has any evidence yet been made public that the new ship will feature characteristics necessary for such operations—catapults and arresting gear. United States Navy sources have speculated, however, that the ship is designed to operate vertical or short takeoff and landing (V/STOL) aircraft. These reports are based on the size of the vessel and on the apparent length and angle of its flight deck, which would not be necessary if only helicopter operations were envisioned. It is also known that the Soviet Navy recently began flight-testing V/STOL aircraft. Conceivably, however, the ship could be used solely for helicopter operations, such as has been the case for the Moskva class. Several important deficiencies in V/STOL technology argue for such an outcome.

Speculation as to possible functions of the new ship encompass a wide variety of possibilities. On the one hand, some believe that it may be simply a successor of the Moskva, carrying helicopters designed for antisubmarine operations. Others argue that the new ship will more probably be intended for, and carry helicopters designed for, assault operations. Still others believe that the ship will carry V/STOL aircraft, which could be designed for antisubmarine

62. Zumwalt letter of June 2, p. 5.

63. *Time,* Jan. 21, 1972; *New York Times,* Oct. 17, 1972; *Jane's Fighting Ships, 1972-73,* pp. 79-80, 576; artist's sketch with accompanying caption released by Secretary of Defense Melvin R. Laird, January 1973; *New York Times,* Feb. 27, 1973.

64. An estimated 23,000 to 25,000 tons as against an actual 18,000 tons full-load displacement. *New York Times,* Oct. 23, 1967, and Feb. 14, 1968. The fact that public reports about the new ship first appeared so long before its completion could indicate either improvements in U.S. intelligence capabilities or the greater importance of the Soviet Navy for budget-related politics in the United States.

warfare, for close-in air defense of Soviet surface vessels, or for air-strike operations.

The new ship's function is not solely a question of the type of aircraft to be deployed on it. Design characteristics of the vessel itself will partially determine such possibilities. For example, if the ship is intended as an assault vessel, it will incorporate cargo storage facilities for tanks and other large items of equipment, will have troop accommodations, and so forth. Unfortunately, currently available information on these characteristics is too scanty to permit reasoned judgments as to which of the above possibilities is more probable.

The appearance of a full-fledged aircraft carrier would be a momentous event in the evolution of Soviet naval power. On the assumption that it was not simply a case of imitating the United States by building a large ship for prestige and other nonwarfare purposes, its appearance could well presage an upgrading of the priority accorded the projection mission and other forms of surface operations. Such a decision would not be taken lightly by the Soviet Union, however, as it implies enormous costs in both investment and operating expenses. Not only would the carriers themselves have to be built, but their specialized equipment (for example, arresting gear and catapults) would have to be developed. Moreover, carrier operations require aircraft with special characteristics (such as folding wings and strengthened undercarriages) that would have to be designed and procured. Finally, a large number of Soviet seamen and pilots would have to be trained in skills very different from those currently employed in Soviet naval operations.

As has been noted, the mystery ship at Nikolaev is unlikely to have all the features of modern U.S. aircraft carriers. Nonetheless, if it is designed for other than helicopter-borne antisubmarine operations, it indicates continuing evolution of Soviet capabilities toward such an end. This implies two things: a new direction in Soviet conceptions of the utility of sea power, and the resolution, at least for the time being, of the internal debate in the Soviet Union in the direction of those who view the advantages of providing their surface naval forces with sea-based air power as being worth the incremental costs.

Conclusions

In the nearly twenty years since the reevaluation of Soviet naval strategy and force structure that followed Stalin's death, the Soviet Union has developed a modern "blue-water" navy of major proportions, a force fully capable of attaining many of the specific objectives that have been set out for it. The

USSR has developed and deployed a fleet of ballistic missile submarines with capabilities comparable, if still qualitatively inferior, to their U.S. counterparts. It has built a relatively small number of surface warships of ultramodern design—ships that have dazzled the West by their design efficiency, their firepower, and their propulsion and electronic systems. It has built a much larger force of smaller surface vessels and has deployed a large number of land-based aircraft for the defense of waters contiguous to the USSR. It is constructing a large force of nuclear-powered attack and cruise missile submarines that could present severe problems to U.S. naval task forces and to U.S. and allied merchant shipping in the event of hostilities. Finally, the Soviet Union has increasingly deployed its navy to regions distant from its home waters and has maintained standing naval forces in regions of traditional Western maritime domination.

All of this, however, should not obscure the fact that Soviet naval capabilities have developed not as a result of increasing force levels, but rather as a consequence of improvements in individual unit capabilities and of an expansion in the scope of the navy's peacetime role. Moreover, capabilities have been improved selectively, with some missions emphasized and others largely neglected. Generally, and with the exception of strategic submarines, the Soviet Navy does not appear to be designed to project the Soviet Union's power into distant oceans but to defend the security and interests of the USSR—by preventing attacks on its homeland and by limiting the role of the United States and other Western powers in regions close to Soviet shores, notably the Middle East. The Soviet Navy's past building programs, its exercises, its peacetime deployments, and Soviet military doctrine all support the assessment that the primary emphasis in Soviet naval evolution has been and is likely to remain oriented to the accomplishment of these missions.

This does not mean that the Soviet Navy would not engage in time of war in interdiction and in the other missions currently given low priority, for reasons indicated previously, but several factors limit the degree and the effectiveness with which such missions could be undertaken. The Soviet Navy has little capability for intervening overseas in the face of military opposition, having neither fixed-wing aircraft based at sea nor sizable amphibious assault forces. It would have difficulty supporting sustained surface operations on the high seas as it lacks an overseas infrastructure, has inadequate support forces, and has not designed its combat vessels for protracted wars at sea. Despite its best efforts and the deployment of relatively large numbers of antisubmarine systems, the Soviet Navy's capabilities against modern quiet-running submarines appear to be limited. Its equipment, ordnance, sensors, tactics, and various operational procedures are probably not designed for large-scale antishipping campaigns.

As indicated in the previous section, however, the Soviet Navy may now be at a turning point. The Soviet Union is a nation just like any other, with finite resources, and consequently faces difficult choices both about the amount of funds and manpower it should allocate to its navy and about the distribution of resources within the navy itself. While these choices will be made on the basis of a wide variety of factors, considerable attention is likely to be paid to the capabilities and intentions of the Soviet Union's foremost potential adversary—the United States.[65]

At the present time the U.S. Navy is in the midst of a major modernization program. The fiscal 1974 budget requests a real increase of more than $1 billion in Navy baseline (non-Vietnam) investment—procurement, shipbuilding, construction, and research and development. More broadly, Navy baseline investment for fiscal 1972 through fiscal 1974 will average 23 percent more, again in real terms, than the comparable figures for the previous four years. The other military services will show a 14 percent real decrease in baseline investment over the same time period. Shipbuilding funds alone have more than tripled since their fiscal 1969 low; they are currently 50 percent higher than the 1962-69 average.

In part, these increased spending levels have resulted from the need to modernize the aging American fleet and to replace many vessels commissioned during and shortly after World War II. In part, they have resulted from estimates of the force required to carry out missions unrelated to U.S.-Soviet conflict. Also, however, large dollar allocations for naval modernization are predicated on improvements in Soviet naval capabilities. For example, Admiral Thomas H. Moorer, chairman of the Joint Chiefs of Staff, stated:

> The problem we face with the continuing growth in Soviet naval capabilities relative to our own is a matter of increasing concern to the Joint Chiefs of Staff. . . . Unless we accelerate the modernization of our fleet, the Soviets will increasingly challenge our control of the seas in those maritime regions essen-

65. For an example of Soviet attentiveness to and interpretations of U.S. naval developments, see B. L. Teplinskiy, "The World Ocean and U.S. Military Strategy," *USA: Economics, Politics, Ideology,* No. 10 (September 1972), pp. 15-24, translated in Foreign Broadcast Information Service, *Daily Report: Soviet Union* (Oct. 18, 1972), pp. H1-11. For a historical overview of Soviet reactions to U.S. naval evolution, see Thomas W. Wolfe, *Soviet Naval Interaction with the United States and Its Influence on Soviet Naval Development,* Paper P-4913 (Santa Monica: RAND Corp., October 1972).

tial to the success of our forward defense strategy, as well as in the ocean areas closer to our shores.[66]

Thus, while estimates of Soviet naval capabilities are not the sole or even necessarily the dominant factor in decisions about the size and composition of the U.S. Navy, it is clear that such estimates do play a role in U.S. naval planning. This makes it important to examine in depth changes in the Soviet Navy—to understand what they are and what they are intended to achieve. And as part of such an evaluation, one should consider the relative priorities the Soviet Union places on the various potential missions of its fleets.

Current priorities are not a sure guide to future decisions, particularly in time of conflict. Since intentions can change a good deal more rapidly than capabilities, military planners naturally prefer to hedge against all contingencies. Still, a response that also takes account of intentions—as evidenced by ship construction and retirement programs, weapons and sensor procurement, exercises, statements by military and political leaders, and other types of empirical data—can help accomplish several important objectives. It may help reduce the cost of the continuing U.S.-Soviet naval rivalry, particularly if it strengthens those in the USSR who prefer both to reallocate resources from the military to the civilian sectors and to stabilize the military balance between the great powers in the field of general purpose forces. Evidence as to how and why Soviet force structure decisions are reached is too fragmentary to give complete assurance, however, that such U.S. responses would have this effect. More important, this kind of response could help to avoid a situation in which the United States winds up with a naval force primarily designed to meet the "worst" conceivable contingency but poorly structured to act in situations that are more likely to be encountered.

Specifically, one should recognize the divergences between the potential "war-fighting" capability of the Soviet Navy and its actual use as an instrument of foreign policy during peacetime. The two superpowers are engaged in a naval rivalry. The driving force behind this rivalry is not, however, the fear that one side or the other will achieve sufficient military advantage to initiate large-scale conflict. So long as the threat of escalation to nuclear war looms over any potential U.S.-Soviet military engagement, the probability of a shooting war between the superpowers will remain small. Rather, both sides are motivated by fear of the political consequences of any apparently sharp change to the relative naval balance. The United States has long enjoyed a position of overwhelming naval superiority. The fear is that some nations,

66. *Statement on Department of Defense Appropriations FY 1973,* Pt. 1, p. 29.

perceiving the naval (and more general military) balance to be turning toward the Soviet Union, would be reluctant to associate themselves with the United States, would make concessions to the Soviet Union inimical to U.S. interests, and would eventually draw closer to the Soviet orbit. Beyond this, there is concern that growing Soviet naval capabilities may increase Soviet willingness to take risks in bringing pressure to bear on other countries and may diminish U.S. willingness to assume comparable risks.

The extent to which these concerns are well founded is difficult to judge. There are few data dealing with the political consequences of naval acquisitions and deployments; concerns such as those expressed above are based on supposition. That the potential political effect of these factors is likely to be subtle and intangible compounds the difficulty. To a certain extent, moreover, the way foreign nations perceive the trend in the naval balance is a result of what U.S. policy makers and other prominent world figures say about it. If the United States stresses the *military* threat posed by the Soviet Navy (and budgetary considerations often prompt such an emphasis), the *political* consequences of that naval force can be expected to be magnified. This is not to say that political consequences are imaginary or that a nation's political fortunes are not related to an "objective" assessment of its relative military capabilities—merely that the relationship is not a direct one and that there are intervening variables.

As the U.S. Navy does not have unlimited resources, investments in ships, weapons, or other equipment primarily designed to counter missions of relatively low priority to the Soviet Union could detract from the U.S. ability to carry out necessary missions in more likely contingencies. This point should not be carried too far, as naval forces are inherently flexible. Nonetheless, differences in the types of weapons, in tactics, in the characteristics of sensors, and in the preferred design of ships and aircraft are dependent on what is envisioned as those systems' primary purposes.

The foregoing analysis is not intended to support any specific size or composition of the U.S. Navy. The evidence presented here is not sufficiently detailed for this purpose. The analysis does, however, suggest certain judgments about Soviet mission intentions which bear on U.S. force planning.

There is sufficient uncertainty about the degree and imminence of the threat posed by the Soviet Navy to Western sea lines of communication to raise questions as to whether countering this threat should have a high priority in the allocation of U.S. Navy resources. On the other hand, there is sufficient evidence about increasing emphasis on the peacetime and crisis use of the Soviet Navy for political purposes to suggest a need for ensuring that U.S.

forces are fully capable of accomplishing the missions set out for them as instruments of naval diplomacy—both in projecting U.S. power and influence and in countering the Soviet Union's efforts to project its own influence. While the political consequences of the use of naval forces in these situations are likely to depend on not only the local balance of naval force, but also the broad strategic balance and the general context of political relations within and among the nations involved, the size and capabilities of rival navies will be considered by both potential adversaries and third parties as major determinants of their own behavior. Hence the requirements for effective political use of the fleet in peacetime and in crises should have high priority in U.S. naval force planning.

Comparing the U.S. and Soviet Navies

In the halcyon days before the advent of nuclear warheads, ballistic and cruise missiles, long-range aircraft, electronic warfare measures and countermeasures, and the other appurtenances of modern technology, comparisons of the naval power of various nations were relatively simple matters. Each state owned so many warships in several classes; each could field so many guns of various calibers on those vessels. Although more qualitative differences certainly existed—leadership, armor, gunner's accuracy—they were not such that their effect was considered likely to overwhelm any but the most narrow quantitative imbalances. Consequently, questions about the adequacy of a naval force could be answered relatively easily, by simple force level comparisons with those of potential adversaries.

Though they continue to have intuitive appeal, such comparisons are no longer meaningful indices of relative naval power. Usually simplistic, they are frequently irrelevant to questions of force level adequacy and are at times quite misleading.

This is particularly the case for the naval forces of the United States and the Soviet Union. In aggregate, the U.S. force is much larger. In terms of active-duty military manpower, for example, the U.S. Navy is at least one-fifth larger (602,000 as against 500,000) and two-thirds larger if one includes the Coast Guard and the Marine Corps in the U.S. total.[1] The U.S. force is certainly the more expensive one. At U.S. prices, annual Soviet naval costs probably amount to about half U.S. Navy costs.

Yet the two forces are so fundamentally different that the consequences of this difference for the ability of each state to achieve the objectives of its naval deployments are not readily apparent. Table A-1 contains simple comparisons of force levels and of significant measures of capability. The U.S. Navy clearly has an advantage in projection forces. While the Soviet Union

---

1. Manpower data taken from R. V. B. Blackman (ed.), *Jane's Fighting Ships, 1972-73* (London: Jane's Yearbooks, 1972). Soviet equivalents of the Marines and the Coast Guard are included in the 500,000 figure.

Table A-1. Comparative Force Levels, 1972

Component	Number[a] U.S.	Number[a] USSR	Measure of capability Item	Measure of capability U.S.	Measure of capability USSR
Strategic submarines					
Nuclear	41	35	Missile launchers	656	443
Conventional	0	20	Missile launchers	0	60
Units used mainly for inter-ventionary missions					
Fixed-wing aircraft carriers	14	0			
Tactical air wings[b]	15	0			
Assault helicopter carriers	7	0	Full-load displacement[c]	128	–
Other amphibious warfare vessels[d]	68	100	Full-load displacement[c]	828	146
Marines (thousands of men)	198	15			
Major surface warships					
ASW carriers, fixed wing	3	0			
ASW carriers, helicopter	0	2			
Cruisers/frigates	39	28	Missile launchers, surface-to-air	118	46
			Missile launchers, surface-to-surface	0	88
Destroyers/escorts	188	193	Missile launchers, surface-to-air	46	104
			Missile launchers, surface-to-surface	0	24
Attack submarines					
Nuclear	57	65	Missile launchers	0	288
			Torpedo tubes	269	426
Conventional	41	225	Missile launchers	0	102
			Torpedo tubes	386	1,484
Patrol vessels					
Missile patrol boats	0	150			
All others[e]	160	500			
Land-based aircraft					
Strike, tanker, and reconnais-sance aircraft[f]	0	500			
ASW patrol aircraft	300	100			
Mine warfare vessels					
Ocean-going	31	195			
Coastal	0	125			
Support ships					
Underway replenishment	83	0			
Fleet and logistic support	91	n.a.			

Sources: Data derived from R. V. B. Blackman (ed.), *Jane's Fighting Ships, 1972-73;* Letter, Admiral E. R. Zumwalt, Jr., to Senator William Proxmire, June 2, 1972, reprinted in *Congressional Record* (June 12, 1972), pp. S9186-92; *Statement of Secretary of Defense Melvin R. Laird on Department of Defense Appropriations FY 1973,* Hearings before the Senate Appropriations Committee, 92 Cong. 2 sess. (1972), Pt. 1, p. 70.

Table A-1, *notes (continued)*

n.a. Not available.
a. Estimated number in active-duty force at mid-1972.
b. Includes three Marine Corps wings.
c. Thousand tons.
d. Excludes landing craft.
e. All but 37 of the U.S. vessels are assigned to the Coast Guard.
f. Includes only aircraft operated by U.S. and USSR naval forces.

has only a token force of marines and amphibious vessels, aircraft carriers and amphibious assault forces occupy a central position in the U.S. Navy's force structure. In major surface warships, the two sides are relatively evenly balanced, at least in numbers of units. Aside from numbers of missile launchers, however, the table does not portray differences in the capabilities of weapon systems or, for that matter, in the characteristics of propulsion systems, electronics, or sensors.

The Soviet Navy has a major advantage in total number of attack submarines, although the two navies are relatively evenly balanced in the number of nuclear-propelled units. Other major Soviet advantages can be seen in patrol vessels and mine warfare ships. The USSR has a large land-based force of strike aircraft, whereas the United States has no land-based strike aircraft assigned to its maritime forces.[2] Conversely, the USSR has only makeshift underway replenishment ships (except for submarine support) and a much smaller service force in general.

There are other important differences between the two navies that are not shown in the table. First, the United States has a large network of land bases in foreign nations supporting its naval deployments; the Soviet Union has only a few minor facilities. Also, U.S. ships tend to be much larger than their Soviet counterparts. In the destroyer/escort category, for example, U.S. units are about 25 percent larger on the average than equivalent Soviet vessels (2,600 tons opposed to 2,100 tons, standard displacement). The factors that lead to this difference—better habitability for American crews, greater endurance and reload capacity for U.S. vessels—presumably would confer certain advantages on the U.S. side in the event of a confrontation. Conversely, the Soviet Navy has the advantage in the average age of the two fleets. Table A-2 shows that, whereas both nations seem to have built similar portions of their fleets within the past nine years, the Soviet Union constructed a much larger part of its navy during the last ten to nineteen years than did the United States. These relative proportions will soon be changing, however, as both sides are now retiring large numbers of older ships.

2. U.S. Air Force bombers could be used for antiship missions if they were not required for other purposes at the same time. Secretary Laird has indicated that in consonance with the "total force approach," the Air Force has been developing tactics and training for such operations. See *Statement of Secretary of Defense Melvin R. Laird on Department of Defense Appropriations FY 1973,* Hearings before the Senate Appropriations Committee, 92 Cong. 2 sess. (1972), Pt. 1.

Table A-2. Comparative Age of Major Units in the U.S. and Soviet Navies, Active Ships as of July 1, 1972

In percent

Type of ship	Under 10 years		10-19 years		20 years or more	
	U.S.	USSR	U.S.	USSR	U.S.	USSR
Strategic submarines	76	58	24	42	0	0
Attack aircraft carriers	14	n.a.	50	n.a.	36	n.a.
Amphibious warfare ships[a]	64	74	34	26	2	0
ASW carriers[b]	0	100	0	0	100	0
Cruisers/frigates	46	46	32	32	22	22
Destroyers/escorts	32	39	25	51	43	10
Cruise missile submarines	n.a.	74	n.a.	26	n.a.	0
Torpedo attack submarines	45	22	22	78	33	0
Mine warfare ships	64	47	34	44	2	9
All major units	45	45	28	50	27	5

Source: Department of the Navy, Office of the Chief of Naval Operations (OP-906D), "Memorandum for the Chief of Legislative Affairs, May 5, 1972."
    n.a. Not applicable.
    a. Excludes landing craft.
    b. Fixed-wing aircraft for the United States; helicopters for the Soviet Union.

Finally, in an assessment of the consequences of these and other differences to the capacity of each navy to attain its objectives, other secondary factors come into play. For example, the significance of age differences should be tempered by any differences between the two navies' maintenance policies or in the extent to which each has modernized equipment on older vessels. Clearly, an older ship that is well maintained and modernized at regular intervals can be as effective as a younger counterpart. Similarly, size differences must be modified by comparisons of design efficiency.

These major differences between the Navy of the USSR and that of the United States are not coincidental, of course. They reflect differences in the two states' geographic positions, in their respective conceptions of their role in world affairs, in their historic experiences, in their views of the importance and function of sea power, in the resources each has been willing to allocate to its maritime forces at any given time, and many other factors. The net effect, however, is to make real comparisons of the two navies difficult to accomplish.

In a remarkable demonstration of concurrence, this has been attested to by the Commanders-in-Chief of both the U.S. and Soviet Navies. Admiral S. G. Gorshkov wrote:

The qualitative transformations which have taken place in naval forces have also changed the approach to evaluating the relative might of navies and their combat groupings: we have had to cease comparing the number of warships of one type or another, and their total displacement (or the number of guns in a salvo or the weight of this salvo) and turn to a more complex, but also more correct appraisal of the striking and defensive power of ships based on a mathematical analysis of their capabilities and qualitative characteristics.[3]

Six months later, Admiral Zumwalt wrote on the same topic:

direct comparison of force levels or unit tonnage can lead to clearly erroneous conclusions regarding the relative capabilities of the two sides. This simplistic and outmoded approach to the complex process of "net assessment" was abandoned as inadequate by competent specialists in the field many years ago.[4]

Unfortunately, it is extremely difficult to perform this type of dynamic mathematical analysis, or net assessment. The pertinent interactions are numerous and complex, the critical factors difficult to isolate and quantify, and simulation models required are lengthy to run, time consuming to construct, and difficult to manage. In addition to problems stemming from requirements of specialized expertise and extensive computing facilities, the difficulties in analysis are compounded by its being heavily dependent on information about the technical specifications of weapons, sensors, and other types of hardware. Without detailed estimates of these factors, which are usually quite closely held by the governments concerned, such analyses can be only exercises designed to test the boundaries of the situation.

The purpose of this appendix is more modest: to inform the reader which comparisons of U.S.-Soviet naval power are most meaningful. Consequently, several scenarios are presented, each of which describes a way in which the U.S. and Soviet Navies might come into conflict. Through these scenarios, the nature and content of relevant force comparisons become evident. For each scenario, the numbers and types of forces that could be brought into play on each side are described. Pertinent forces of allies also are mentioned. Scenarios involving the use of strategic forces are omitted, as is any assessment of the probable outcome of the conflicts, which is beyond the scope of this analysis.

In the United States, discussions of the manner in which the U.S. and Soviet Navies might come into conflict with one another tend to focus on three broad scenarios: (a) a Soviet campaign to interdict Western merchant shipping; (b) a Soviet attempt to interpose forces in a situation where the United States was intervening in a conflict overseas; and (c) a war between the two superpowers limited to the seas. Although these three do not exhaust the range of possible interactions, and despite the fact that at the margins they tend to blend into one another, they have in their many variations formed the basis of informed discussions of the comparative capabilities of the two naval forces. Discussion in the Soviet Union, however, is likely to have been differ-

3. "Navies in Wars and in Peace," *Morskoi Sbornik,* No. 2 (February 1972), p. 21.
4. Letter from Admiral E. R. Zumwalt, Jr., to Senator William Proxmire, June 2, 1972, reprinted in *Congressional Record* (June 12, 1972), p. S9187.

ently oriented, with the possible exception of the second scenario indicated above, for reasons related to the Soviet conception of the primary mission of its navy—strategic defense. Nonetheless, the three U.S.-favored scenarios are convenient mechanisms for planning purposes.

Soviet Interdiction Campaigns

For many years, estimates of the threat posed by the Soviet Union to the maritime interests of the United States and its allies usually focused on the potential use of the Soviet submarine fleet against merchant and military support shipping, primarily in the Atlantic. Attention to this was given impetus by the enormous diesel-powered attack-submarine building program undertaken by the Soviet Union around 1950. Also a factor was the tendency to discount the possibility that the Soviet Union might want such a large number of vessels simply to counter U.S. aircraft carriers, which were then cast primarily in a strategic role. Interdiction campaigns are usually envisioned in connection with a protracted conventional war in Europe. Consequently, the credibility accorded this scenario is dependent, in large part, on the seriousness with which the likelihood of large-scale conventional war of substantial duration is viewed.

To carry out an interdiction campaign the Soviet Union has available some 225 torpedo attack submarines, of which 28 are nuclear-powered. If submarines assigned to the Pacific and Black Sea Fleets and those laid up for overhauls or other disabilities are subtracted from this number, there would be 100 to 150 torpedo attack submarines for interdiction missions in the Atlantic and the Mediterranean. In addition, some portion of the Soviet Union's 65 cruise missile-equipped submarines also could be used in interdiction missions. The precise number depends on one's assessment of the number of cruise missile and torpedo attack submarines the USSR would assign to warship targets, and the percentage of those that could be expected to survive these engagements. One variant of the interdiction scenario envisions the USSR's use of its naval air force to supplement submarine attacks. To this end, the Soviet Union has available some 300 Tu-16 (Badger) strike aircraft equipped with air-to-surface missiles. Again, however, first priority for these forces would be warship targets; only the aircraft that survived these engagements could be used against shipping.

To counter these threats, NATO can array a variety of forces. Through the use of data developed from various underwater detection systems, submarine contacts could be prosecuted by both land- and sea-based antisubmarine warfare (ASW) aircraft. This type of operation is known as area search. The United States has some twenty-four squadrons of P-3 maritime patrol aircraft, most of which would be available for Atlantic or Mediterranean operations. In addition, the other NATO states can contribute roughly twenty maritime air patrol squadrons of varied types (Atlantic, Nimrod, Argus, Tracker, and P-2).[5] In mid-1972, the United States also had three ASW aircraft carriers equipped with S-2 aircraft, but this force will be phased out by mid-1974. On the other hand, the United States will have begun to operate more modern ASW aircraft, S-3, from attack carriers.

NATO would also establish barriers along potential routes that would be used by Soviet submarines in passage between their home bases and the shipping lanes. Mines could be used in some areas, submarines and aircraft in others. In mid-1972, the United States had more than fifty nuclear attack submarines that could be used for these purposes. The U.S. inventory also included forty diesel-powered submarines. The other NATO states had an additional hundred submarines. Only six of these (U.K.) were nuclear-powered, however, and many of the diesel-powered boats would be of limited use.

Another form of NATO submarine defense is that provided directly to shipping. These local or point defenses, consisting of surface escorts and perhaps ship-based helicopters, can be used when shipping is routed in convoys, as in World War II. Requirements for the protection of aircraft carriers and other high-value military targets leave the United States with little escort capacity to spare for convoy work, unless reserve units are activated and function effectively. American allies in NATO, however, could supply roughly 200 ocean-going escorts of various types and degrees of effectiveness. As an alternative to convoys, the West could adopt the tactic of routing ships singly, protecting them by attempting to maintain a sort of moving barrier along the shipping lanes, using surface escorts, submarines, and/or aircraft for these purposes.

NATO would have a number of options against the threat provided by Soviet land-based aircraft. Land- and carrier-based aircraft would attempt to interdict Soviet strike aircraft before they reached their targets. Surface escorts equipped with surface-to-air missiles would be used as a final point defense against the air threat if ships were sailed in convoys. Rerouting shipping would also aid in diminishing the air threat, at least in the Atlantic, since the range of Soviet aircraft is limited. This assumes that the Soviet Union would be deterred from overflying extensive NATO land-based air defenses in Europe.

Two other forms of interdiction campaigns are also worth mentioning.

One envisions a conflict as described above but independent of a possible land war in Europe. In this scenario, the Soviet Union might consider undertaking such a campaign either in response to Western political or military

5. Unless otherwise noted, data on the force levels of NATO states are taken from International Institute for Strategic Studies, *The Military Balance, 1972-73* (London: IISS, 1972).

actions it considered provocative or as a means of extending its influence in Western Europe. Proponents of this scenario stress that dependence on maritime trade makes the Western alliance especially vulnerable to such measures and that avoiding a land war is advantageous to the USSR. It is generally assumed that the course of the war would evolve in a manner similar to that described above.

The second variant foresees a more limited form of interdiction. In it, the Soviet Union would attempt to compel or deter a Western action by staging sporadic, and possibly covert, submarine attacks on valuable maritime resources, for example, on supertankers. By demonstrating the West's vulnerability to interdiction in this manner, the USSR would hope to wrest concessions in some related area.

Intervention and Interposition

Scenarios envisioning a Soviet attempt to prevent or end U.S. intervention in a conflict overseas most frequently involve the Mediterranean. The particulars of these scenarios can vary a great deal, depending on whether the United States is actually engaged in land operations when the conflict with the USSR erupts and, if so, of what type; the degree to which each side has reinforced its normal Mediterranean deployments before the hostilities; the participation of allied states (particularly U.S. allies); and other factors. In all cases, however, the outcome depends on the success or failure of Soviet attacks on the U.S. Sixth Fleet.

The Sixth Fleet typically consists of some forty to fifty vessels including the flagship (a cruiser), two aircraft carriers, each with six to eight escorts, an amphibious assault force of six ships carrying a Marine battalion landing team, two to three submarines, several minesweepers, and underway replenishment ships and other auxiliaries. This force can be reinforced fairly rapidly with units from the Second Fleet deployed in the Atlantic. At the time of the Jordanian crisis in 1970, for example, the United States put an additional carrier task force, an amphibious assault helicopter carrier, and other units into the Mediterranean within a short time. If bases are available, the United States can also make use of land-based aircraft. Three to six U.S. fighter-interceptor squadrons are always available in Spain, Italy, or Turkey. Others can be flown to Mediterranean bases from their normal bases elsewhere in Europe. The number of these that would be assigned to a Mediterranean conflict and the number that could be accommodated at local facilities is not clear, however.

Depending on the precise reason for and location of the intervention, the forces of various other states could be added to the U.S. total. At maximum,

these forces could include several helicopter carriers, fifty or so surface warships, and around thirty submarines. And states on the Mediterranean littoral
could make a significant contribution of land-based aircraft. Again, however,
this would depend on the exact nature of the conflict.

The Soviet Mediterranean squadron consists, typically, of fifty to sixty
vessels. Admiral Zumwalt has released figures showing the numbers and types
of ships making up the Soviet force:[6]

	Number of units	
Type of ship	Observed on a typical day	Largest number observed in one day
Helicopter carriers	0	2
Cruisers	2	6
Destroyers and escorts	5	17
Attack and cruise missile submarines	9	22

The precise number and characteristics of Soviet units will also depend on the
warning period leading up to the crisis and, once hostilities have begun, on
the degree of success the United States has in gaining control of the key straits
leading into the Mediterranean. The USSR would also make use of land-based
aircraft in these crises. Long-range reconnaissance aircraft would be used to
help locate the major units of the Sixth Fleet. Subsequently, land-based strike
aircraft carrying air-to-surface missiles would be employed against major fleet
units. Most of these aircraft are based within the USSR near the Black Sea.
The Soviet Union's access to land bases on the periphery of the Mediterranean,
such as those it had until July 1972 in Egypt, would greatly increase its capabilities in this regard.

The course and outcome of the battle would depend on the precise details
of the scenario, the amount of surprise one or the other side could attain, the
actual performance of various weapons and sensor systems, and many other
considerations. In essence, the Soviet Union would attempt to use its air-to-
surface-missile-carrying aircraft, submarines (particularly those equipped with
cruise missiles), and surface-to-surface-missile-equipped surface warships to
attack U.S. interventionary forces—particularly aircraft carriers. If the United
States were already intervening when the Soviet Union initiated hostilities,
the latter would have one advantage in that the U.S. forces actually engaged
in the land campaign would be confined to a small area. The USSR would
probably also deploy submarines to the so-called choke points in the Mediterranean—near Gibraltar, the straits between Italy, Sicily, and North Africa, and
elsewhere—in attempts to interdict Western reinforcements.

The United States would use land- and sea-based aircraft to attack Soviet

6. Letter from Admiral E. R. Zumwalt, Jr., to Senator William Proxmire, June 8,
1972, p. 5; reprinted in *Congressional Record* (June 12, 1972), p. S9194.

surface units. Soviet submarines would be attacked by ASW escort ships, sea-based ASW aircraft if available, and the two squadrons of U.S. maritime patrol aircraft typically deployed to the Mediterranean. Against the Soviet force of land-based strike aircraft, the United States would rely on surface-to-air missiles on escort ships, and on land-based air defenses if the Soviet Union chose to overfly areas in which they were available.

Wars at Sea

Some analysts point to wars limited to the sea as the more likely form of combat between the United States and the Soviet Union. According to this argument, the advent of parity in strategic forces and growth of the Soviet Union's naval power have altered the environment of U.S.-Soviet interactions. It is maintained that strategic parity prevents conflicts from escalating beyond limited war and that the unique characteristics of wars at sea make the oceans a more likely arena for limited U.S.-Soviet conflict. Wars are said to be inherently easier to limit at sea because of the greater physical separation between combatants and civilians, the greater decisiveness of battles at sea, the greater control political leaders could exercise on combatants at sea, and the greater flexibility of naval units.[7]

On the other hand, many dispute the credibility of naval wars between the United States and the Soviet Union. From this viewpoint, the costs associated with strategic nuclear war are so great, regardless of questions of parity or imbalance, that any measure implying a serious risk of escalation is unlikely to be adopted. Because major naval vessels are of such great value—in crew size and cost—neither nation could sink one without undertaking a great risk of escalation. The backdrop of potential strategic nuclear war between the superpowers would inhibit the actual use of naval vessels in conflicts with one another. According to this view, aside from their use against third parties, the naval forces of the two great powers serve largely symbolic purposes: to signal interest and intentions, to serve as a trip wire for national commitments, and to weigh, for political purposes, in calculations of the military balance.

The expected course of a war-at-sea scenario is not at all clear. Presumably, it would center upon Soviet efforts to sink or damage U.S. aircraft carriers and U.S. defensive efforts to prevent such an occurrence. The Soviet Union does not offer any comparable targets for U.S. offensive efforts. At most, U.S. submarines and carrier-based aircraft could attempt to find and destroy the limited number of major Soviet warships. Given this disparity in single targets,

7. For more complete arguments along these lines see Desmond P. Wilson and Nicholas Brown, *Warfare at Sea: Threat of the Seventies,* Professional Paper 79 (Arlington, Va.: Center for Naval Analyses, 1971).

it is likely that a U.S. president would be hard-pressed to refrain from responding to the loss of a carrier with an attack on Soviet land targets. This would be particularly true if the carrier had been damaged by land-based aircraft.

Other elements likely to enter into a war at sea would be a Soviet interdiction campaign on the order of that discussed above, and U.S. efforts to mine or otherwise close the narrow straits which dominate three of the four Soviet fleet areas. To counter this, the USSR might consider using its small naval infantry and amphibious force to seize contiguous territory. It could also make use of its large number of patrol vessels in attempts to retain control of nearby fleet areas; its 150 missile-armed patrol boats might prove particularly useful in this task.